Black Students
and
School Failure

Recent Titles in
Contributions in Afro-American and African Studies

Visible Now: Blacks in Private Schools
Diana T. Slaughter and Deborah J. Johnson, editors

Feel the Spirit: Studies in Nineteenth-Century Afro-American Music
George R. Keck and Sherrill V. Martin, editors

From a Caste to a Minority: Changing Attitudes of American Sociologists Toward
Afro-Americans, 1896 –1945
Vernon J. Williams, Jr.

African-American Principals: School Leadership and Success
Kofi Lomotey

Class and Consciousness: The Black Petty Bourgeoisie in South Africa, 1924 to 1950
Alan Gregor Cobley

Black Novelist as White Racist: The Myth of Black Inferiority in the Novels of Oscar
Micheaux
Joseph A. Young

Capital and the State in Nigeria
John F.E. Ohiorhenuan

Famine in East Africa: Food Production and Food Policies
Ronald E. Seavoy

Archetypes, Imprecators, and Victims of Fate: Origins and Developments of Satire in
Black Drama
Femi Euba

Black and White Racial Identity: Theory, Research, and Practice
Janet E. Helms, editor

BLACK STUDENTS AND SCHOOL FAILURE

Policies, Practices, and Prescriptions

JACQUELINE JORDAN IRVINE

Contributions in Afro-American and African Studies, Number 131

 **GREENWOOD PRESS**
New York • Westport, Connecticut • London

Library of Congress Cataloging-in-Publication Data

Irvine, Jacqueline Jordan.
    Black students and school failure: policies, practices, and
prescriptions / Jacqueline Jordan Irvine.
         p.   cm.—(Contributions in Afro-American and African
studies, ISSN 0069-9624 ; no. 131)
    Includes bibliographical references.
    ISBN 0-313-27215-8 (lib. bdg. : alk. paper)
    1. Afro-Americans—Education. 2. Teacher-student relationships—
United States. 3. Afro-American students—Social conditions.
4. Afro-American students—Economic conditions. I. Title.
II. Title: School failure. III. Series.
LC2771.I77   1990
371.8'2—dc20   89-27162

British Library Cataloguing in Publication Data is available.

Library of Congress Catalog Card Number: 89-27162
ISBN: 0-313-27215-8
ISSN: 0069-9624

First published in 1990

Greenwood Press, Inc.
88 Post Road West, Westport, Connecticut 06881

Printed in the United States of America

The paper used in this book complies with the
Permanent Paper Standard issued by the National
Information Standards Organization (Z39.48-1984).

10 9 8 7 6 5 4 3 2

Copyright Acknowledgments

The author and the publisher gratefully acknowledge the following sources for granting
permission to reprint:

Irvine, J.J. 1986. Teacher-student interactions: Effects of student race, sex, and grade level.
Journal of Educational Psychology, 78(1): 14-21. Copyright © 1986 by the American
Psychological Association. Reprinted by permission of the publisher.

Irvine, J.J. 1988. Disappearing black educators. *The Elementary School Journal* 88(5): 503-13.
Copyright © 1988 by The University of Chicago Press. Reprinted by permission of the
publisher.

Irvine, R.W., and Irvine, J.J. 1983. The impact of the desegregation process on the education of
black students. *The Journal of Negro Education* 52(4): 410-22. Copyright © 1983 by the
Howard University. Reprinted by permission of the publisher.

To my parents, Sara Harris and Eddie Jordan,
and my late grandmother,
Rosie Lee Peabody Harris,
the quintessential advocate of black children

Contents

Illustrations

Tables

Figures

Preface

I am particularly grateful to my family for their love and patience. I must thank my husband, Russell, for his helpful insights and constructive criticism and my daughter, Kelli, whose encouragement and faith in me kept this manuscript alive. My institution, Emory University, granted me a sabbatical to research this work, and my chair, Carole Hahn, and the secretarial staff of the Division of Educational Studies were very supportive throughout this process. To these individuals I am most appreciative.

Finally, I am thankful to all the nameless and faceless black children whose unrealized dreams and unfulfilled potential keep me ever mindful of the tasks I have yet to complete.

Introduction

When the National Commission on Excellence published its well-known report, *A Nation at Risk* (1983), a responsive chord was struck, not only in the educational community but throughout society. The most often-quoted paragraph renders a sharp and startling message:

> The educational foundations of our society are presently being eroded by a rising tide of mediocrity that threatens our very future as a nation and a people. If an unfriendly foreign power had attempted to impose on America the mediocre educational performance that exists today, we might have viewed it as an act of war. As it stands, we have allowed this to happen to ourselves (p. 5).

The nation is indeed at risk, not, however, because Japanese children have higher math scores or Soviet children have longer school days. The nation is at risk because the fastest-growing segment of the school population, blacks and other minorities, is being systematically and effectively excluded from the benefits of educational opportunities. These educational benefits lead to individual economic independence, which this country will ultimately depend upon for its strength and survival.

The current economic, educational, and social condition of black America is dismal, and the outlook for the future seems bleak. The Children's Defense Fund (CDF) (Edelman, 1986) outlined these probabilities:

Compared with white children, black children are two to four times as likely to:

- die before adulthood because of inadequate prenatal or postnatal health care conditions, abuse, or murder;
- live in a single parent household because of parental death, separation, divorce, or no marriage;
- live in foster care or custody of a child welfare agency;
- be poor, living in substandard housing with an unemployed teenage mother.

There is a strong relationship among black student achievement, teen parenthood, and poverty. Poor black students usually score lower on standardized measures of achievement and are overrepresented in the ranks of dropouts and pregnant girls. The CDF (1987) reported that students in the bottom fifth of their classes are more likely to become teen parents than their peers with average skills. It seems that school achievement does play an important role in the prevention of poverty and teen parenthood. The CDF report concluded that "the combination of poverty and weak skills accounts for virtually all of the racial disparities in teen childbearing rates" (p. 4).

In addition to the litany of socioeconomic factors, evidence is mounting that the educational gains of black Americans are being steadily eroded at every level of schooling—elementary, secondary, and higher education. Although black children have shown increased performance on most standardized tests of reading and mathematics, they score significantly lower than whites and Asians. Black seventeen-year-olds show decreased performance in 1980 compared to the 1970s in reading, math, and the sciences, a finding that has led many educators (Coleman, 1966) to observe that the longer black students stay in school, the more likely they are to regress academically.

Perhaps even more telling are the curriculum inequality findings of the College Board (1985) and the *Carnegie Quarterly* (1984/1985). Black students, even if they attend school with whites, receive an education that is different and inferior. The data reveal the following:

- Black students, particularly black male students, are three times as likely to be in a class for the educable mentally retarded as are white students, but only one-half as likely to be in a class for the gifted or talented. For example, in Philadelphia, minorities compose 62 percent of the total enrollment, but only 31 percent of the gifted program serves black students. This underrepresentation can be seen in Prince Georges County, Maryland (49 percent vs.

14 percent), Dade County, Florida (20 percent vs. 5 percent), Duval County, Florida (35 percent vs. 4 percent), and New Orleans (84 percent vs. 26 percent).

- Black students are more likely than white students to be enrolled in general and vocational tracks and take fewer academically rigorous courses. Only 33 percent of blacks are enrolled in college preparatory classes compared to 52 percent of Asians and 40 percent of whites (The College Board, 1985).

- Even though the course titles are similar for black and white students, the content varies (Oakes, 1988). Black students are more likely to be enrolled in business or general math and less likely to be in algebra, geometry, trigonometry, or calculus. In these general courses, students are seldom taught higher-level mathematical skills, and the instruction they do receive emphasizes computation and the recall of facts but rarely critical thinking skills such as problem solving and abstract reasoning (Oakes, 1985). The current instructional focus on the performance-based curriculum makes the already unfortunate situation even more pronounced.

- The National Assessment of Educational Progress (NAEP) compared the reading proficiency levels of black and white youth (NAEP, 1985). Although 53 percent of white eleventh-graders could perform reading tasks that they were likely to encounter in college, only 20 percent of black students could perform these complex reading tasks.

- The relatively recent use of microcomputers in schools has already resulted in quantitative as well as qualitative inequalities. According to a 1984 (Hood) study, schools with 5 percent or fewer students below the poverty level had one microcomputer for every fifty-four students; schools with at least 25 percent of the students below the poverty level had one microcomputer for every seventy-three students. There are qualitative differences as well: Data collected at Johns Hopkins (Becker, 1986) showed that minority students use the computer primarily for drill and practice, as an electronic flash card, which leads these children to perceive that the locus of control lies with the computer—computers tell people what to do. On the other hand, more affluent students, particularly males, learn programming that results in the belief that people tell computers what to do.

Blacks continue to score significantly lower than whites, Hispanics, and Asians on the Scholastic Aptitude Test (SAT). In 1987, blacks scored 351 on the verbal section of this test, compared to the national average score of 430; in mathematics, blacks scored 377 compared to 476 for all other test takers (Rothman, 1987). Bracey (1986) noted that in the past decade, the average SAT scores of blacks have improved by one question each on the SAT verbal and math tests. If this minuscule gain continues at the same pace in the future as it has in the past, and if white test takers' scores do not increase, the average black SAT math score will match that of whites in the year 2045, and the average performance of blacks on the SAT verbal test will equal that of whites in the year 2085.

Particularly alarming are the growing dropout figures for black youngsters. An analysis of the "High School and Beyond" data (National Center for Educational Statistics, 1982) showed that one-half of black and Hispanic high school students who were sophomores in 1980 had dropped out or graduated high-risk by 1984. A high-risk student is one who graduated with a C or lower average (Crawford & Viadero, 1986). These high-risk graduates and dropouts become members of the growing under-class—welfare-dependent and totally alienated from the rest of society. For example, of this 1980 group, 21 percent of the female high-risk students and 58 percent of the female dropouts bore children by 1984.

This lack of achievement and persistence is reflected in the plummeting college attendance rates among middle-class blacks. In 1980, 28 percent of all black students between eighteen and twenty-four years of age enrolled in college. This number had decreased to 19 percent by 1982 (Children's Defense Fund, 1985). When black students do attend college, 42 percent of them attend two-year colleges, where up to 75 percent of entering students leave and never return; fewer than 12 percent complete a four-year degree; and fewer than 5 percent graduate from professional and graduate schools (Baratz, 1986; Zwerling, 1976).

These black students who eventually graduate from four-year colleges leave with economically undervalued degrees in education, the social sciences, and the humanities. When black students do graduate with technically oriented degrees such as those in the sciences, mathematics, and computer sciences, they receive them from historically black rather than white institutions.

Walter Allen (1984) and Jacqueline Fleming (1984) have reported that black students fare better socially, personally, and academically at predominantly black institutions. Allen found that half of the black students entering white institutions never graduate.

Unfortunately, recently enacted programs for educational reform have resulted in yet another blow to the educational achievement of black students. As states call for increased course requirements for graduation, higher grade point averages, longer school days and school years, and passing scores on competency tests, minority students are failing, being retained, and dropping out of schools in record numbers. Eighty percent of the states have some kind of competency testing (Chion-Kenney, 1984), and each day brings more mandated requirements that result in achievement barriers for black students. Edward McDill (1986), of Johns Hopkins's Center for Social Organization of Schools, reported that high-achieving students may profit from these reforms but that tougher standards may force already struggling students to drop out of school. Florida, the state with one of the earliest and most comprehensive programs of competency testing, also has the distinction of being the state with the largest percentage of dropouts (38 percent) in the nation. Researchers (Bondi & Wiles, 1986) predict that when the grade point requirement of 1.5 (of 4.0) for graduation is fully implemented in Florida, the dropout rate will be even greater. When the few educational reform reports include recommendations for high-risk students, they usually take the form of more remediation, which McDill and others have said only reminds struggling students of their failure and ultimately leads to disenchantment and eventual resignation from school.

This discussion and the accompanying data illustrate the severity of the problem of black student achievement. The chapters that follow describe the causes of the problem by presenting a process model that attempts to explain some significant factors that either contribute to or inhibit the school achievement of black students. The model, as depicted in Figure I.1, is primarily grounded in two theories—cultural synchronization and teacher expectancies. Lack of cultural synchronization and negative teacher expectations result in hidden, often unintended, conflict between teachers and their students.

Teacher expectancy theory has roots in theories of classical and instrumental conditioning, learning, achievement motivation, person perception, attribution, and labeling. Robert Merton (1957) was influenced by a statement made by W.I. Thomas (cited in Wilkins, 1976): "If men define situations as real, they are real in their consequences." Merton subsequently developed the concept of the self-fulfilling prophecy. According to Merton, a self-fulfilling prophecy occurs when a false definition of the situation evokes a new behavior that makes the originally false conceptions come true. The false conceptions, Merton believed, cannot be changed by simply providing the perceiver with new knowledge and

Figure I.1
A Process Model for Black Student Achievement

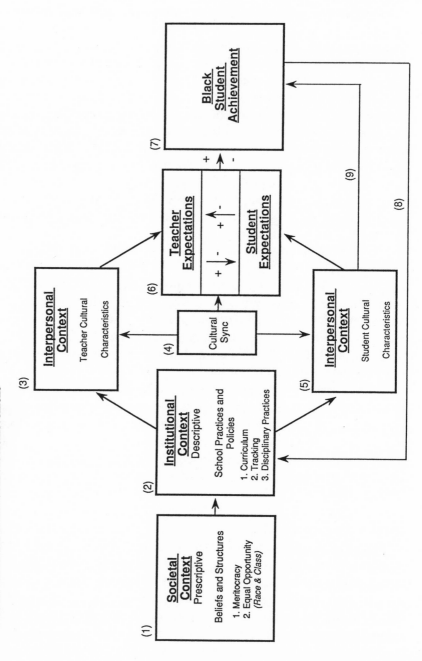

information; changes have to occur in societal structures and norms so that attitudes and behaviors change.

In the application of these theories to schools, the teacher expectancy theory states that teachers form expectations for student achievement and thus treat students differentially because of these expectations. Over time, students begin to behave in ways that are consistent and reinforcing of the teacher's expectations, behavior that results in either positive or negative outcomes related to academic achievement, self-concept, motivation, aspirations, conduct, and teacher-student interactions. The research of Brophy and Evertson (1981), Brophy and Good (1974), Dusek (1985), Oakes (1985), and Persell (1977) is used in the treatment of this section.

Cultural synchronization is rooted in the concepts of Afrocentricity and the cultural distinctiveness of Afro-American life. Afrocentricity is a concept that is associated with an African perspective or center, especially in reference to one's culture and exhibited behaviors. Afrocentricity acknowledges that although American culture can be directly traced to Europe, there are African-Americans whose behaviors are best explained by examining African cultural retentions rather than traditional Eurocentric paradigms. [For a more extensive treatment of this topic, see Asante's (1988) work, "Afrocentricity."] Because the culture of black children is different and often misunderstood, ignored, or discounted, black students are likely to experience cultural discontinuity in schools, particularly schools in which the majority, or Eurocentric persons, control, administer, and teach. The combination of Afrocentric children and Eurocentric schools results in conflict because of lack of cultural correspondence or sync. This lack of cultural sync becomes evident in instructional situations in which teachers misinterpret, denigrate, and dismiss black students' language, nonverbal cues, physical movements, learning styles, cognitive approaches, and worldview. When teachers and students are out of sync, they clash and confront each other, both consciously and unconsciously, in matters concerning proxemics (use of interpersonal distance), paralanguage (behaviors accompanying speech, such as voice tone and pitch and speech rate and length), and coverbal behavior (gesture, facial expression, eye gaze). When black students are in sync with their teachers and school, and no cultural contradictions appear to exist, these children can be expected to be more Eurocentric than Afrocentric in their behavior, attitudes, language, style, and use of standard English and language. Authors who have contributed to the understanding of this theory are Boykin (1986), Hale-Benson (1986), Hilliard (cited in Hale-Benson, 1986), Kochman (1981), Pasteur and Toldson (1982), and Shade (1982), among others.

The model, depicted in Figure I.1, originates from an understanding of the macrolevel of analysis. Within our society there are prescriptive beliefs (1) and prescriptive social structures that are premised on normative belief systems. The principles of meritocracy and equal educational opportunity for children of any race or class are two examples of these "what should be" axioms. Prescriptions are goals and standards that societies use as ways to measure progress and as values to inculcate the young.

These beliefs are operationalized at the descriptive or institutional level (2), where the discrepancy between the prescriptive and the descriptive becomes apparent. Schools have common prescriptive goals, which lack distinctiveness and concreteness—good citizenship, responsibility, literacy, critical thinking skills, computational skills. But the race and the class of the children who attend a particular school, in fact, mediate the observed practices, policies, processes, and organizational structures of that school. For instance, schools that enroll students from lower-class homes often have more bureaucratized structures and are subjected to more rules (Anderson, 1975), have fewer financial resources, have fewer experienced teachers, use a system of rigid tracking, and suspend, expel, and discipline its students more harshly and more often.

At the interpersonal level (3), the roles of teacher and student are defined by the institution. Both teachers and students receive messages from descriptive practices and processes about the behaviors and traits that seem appropriate to the role. Novice teachers learn early, for example, how much academic pressure is expected in a particular school, the degree to which familiarity with students is tolerated, and the role parents play in school decision making. Overt and subtle messages are communicated to students about their ability to succeed, their reliability, and their trustworthiness. Teachers' cultural characteristics (beliefs, attitudes, behaviors, perceptions, worldview), race, sex, social class, prior sex role socialization, education and training, and personality characteristics affect the manner in which the role is enacted. Many low-income black students, however, have a different set of cultural characteristics (5). For black children, their race, class, and culture often act as the normative criteria by which they are initially evaluated by their teacher—not as individuals but as members of their referent group.

The factor of cultural synchronization (4) mediates the interaction of teacher and student in this model. When teachers and black students are in tune culturally, it can be expected that communication is enhanced, instruction is effective, and positive teacher affect is maximized. The presence or the absence of cultural sync influences the interaction of student and teacher expectations (6) both as self-fulfilling prophecies and as sustaining expectation effects. These expectations contribute to or hinder black student achievement (7). The feedback loop in the model (8) reflects the phenomenon in which black students' achievement or non-achievement reinforces the very institutional practices and policies that generated the expectations in the first instance.

The relationship between black students' cultural characteristics and their achievement in school (9) acknowledges that some of the characteristics and behaviors of black students are often in opposition to schools and even the students' own expressed desires to achieve. Weis (1985) noted that the students in her study wanted to go to college and escape poverty but were often absent from school and negligent in their work. She referred to this situation in terms of oppositional cultural forms and believed that these students resisted school because of their understanding of education's limited value in their lives. In an article by Howard and Hammond (1985), black underachievement and the lack of achievement motivation were attributed to black students' acceptance and internalization of society's view that they are unlikely to succeed. Fordham and Ogbu (1986) cited negative peer pressure as inhibiting black achievement. In other words, many black students distrust school and view achievement in school as a white characteristic, and black students who do achieve are ostracized and intimidated by their black peers. The authors recommended programs "to help the students learn to divorce academic pursuit from the idea of acting white" (p. 203).

No model of black student achievement should ignore the fact that there are negative behaviors and attitudes that greatly deter black students' achievement. These maladjustments are often culturally specific and should be addressed by professional educators in the context of the students' home and community.

In the chapters that follow, specific components of the model are examined in more detail.

Chapter 1 posits that schools endorse societal beliefs concerning equal treatment and equality of educational opportunities yet institute and maintain school practices that are conflictual to these beliefs. The hidden curriculum, particularly tracking, is discussed as one such practice.

The conflict between schools' beliefs and their practices is also evidenced at the classroom level. Chapter 2 explores the potential for conflict between teachers and students when there is no or little correspondence or understanding of cultural values, norms, styles, or language. This conflict appears to be related to the declining numbers of black and other minority teachers.

Lack of cultural synchronization because of misunderstanding, missed communications, and low or no teacher-student interaction results in negative teacher expectations. Chapter 3 summarizes the research on teacher expectations and students' expectations for their own success. Three types of expectation studies are reviewed: experimental (non-classroom) studies, teacher perception studies, and naturalistic classroom studies. These studies provide some indication that white teachers have more negative expectations for black students than do black teachers.

Chapter 4 is an original study that discusses the more specific nature of the quality and the quantity of teachers' verbal communications to students as a function of the students' race, gender, and grade level. The research concluded that the white teachers in the study communicated differentially with their students, and there were different patterns of communication and different expectations for black female and black male students.

Chapter 5 focuses on teachers, administrators, and parents. This chapter suggests some interventions for educators of black students who are at risk. This chapter includes a range of strategies such as Afrocentric independent schools, effective teaching, effective schools, and parent education.

Chapter 6 offers competencies that can be developed in teacher training and staff development programs. These competencies are intended as guidelines to be tailored to the individual needs of teachers and schools.

This book claims that black students are subjected to school failure because of their race, social class, and culture. Because these attributes are highly interrelated, it is difficult to disaggregate the complex interplay of these variables at any single moment. This book does not claim that all black children are the same, that is, equally at risk for school failure or manifest behaviors that reflect the operation of an undifferentiated black culture. There are regional, class, and gender variations that must be considered. However, race alone is a salient factor that contributes to unequal school treatment, participation, and distribution of rewards for all black students. Black students, regardless of social class and education, do not share with whites equal opportunities for jobs, housing, and political and economic power. Race, according to Ogbu (1988a), "has its own unique influence on the school experiences and outcomes of black children and similar minorities which is not explained by reference to socioeconomic factors or class struggle" (p. 164).

In all-black school settings, social class, not race, is often the ascendant variable, as evidenced by Rist's (1970) description of black teachers. Surely at other times, black females' lack of school achievement is related to their gender. Whatever the single contributory variable or the interaction between and among variables, there is sufficient evidence that black students' educational and ultimately economic outcomes are influenced by their race, social class, and culture. In summary, black children are not viewed in this book as a monolithic, undifferentiated group; rather, black children are complex products of the polymorphic experiences of black America.

Black Students
and
School Failure

1

Prescriptive Beliefs Versus Descriptive Practices: The Societal and Institutional Contexts

SOCIETAL PRESCRIPTIONS CONCERNING EDUCATION

Prescriptions are primarily societal beliefs that are endorsed by the majority culture. These standards and goals are valued by society and serve as guides or prescriptions for "what should be." Many educators concerned with the educational and social problems of black children direct their energy and expertise toward attaining the prescriptive view, a search for an elusive goal, a hoped-for and anticipated dream, but a never-found reality.

The litany of past and present innovations, strategies, and acronyms is endless—Parent Child Centers, Upward Bound, Chapter I, Head Start, Job Corps, Follow Through, Home Start. These programs, including their

Figure 1.1
Societal Context

Societal Context
Prescriptive

Beliefs and Structures

1. Meritocracy
2. Equal Opportunity
   (Race & Class)

predecessors and progenitors, are primarily the Great Society's compensatory efforts based on beliefs and assumptions that if only the appropriate method, environment, parenting style, money, program, materials, and personnel were implemented, underachieving minority students would catch up with white children. This deficit view assumes that black children, because of cultural, biological, environmental, and social differences, lack the adaptations and knowledge necessary for school achievement.

The educators and policymakers who have a cultural deficit perspective, believe that schools exist primarily to transmit a body of prescribed knowledge, skills, values, and norms that are essential for society. This view deemphasizes the political nature of schooling and its latent agenda for black and other minority students. It assumes that schools serve their students equally and that schools are meritocratic and value-free. Education is thought to provide intellectually able individuals in this society with the appropriate training necessary for employment and occupational opportunities. Education is believed to be positively and directly related to individual and societal productivity and to economic development.

There is an opposing position to this theory of the function of education. Conflict theorists believe that the power of the dominant social group determines economic and educational requirements and that the interest of the powerful is primarily to maintain and reproduce the status quo, which results in a system of inequality for others. These theorists do not search for explanations of black students' lack of achievement by looking at the attributes of programs, interventions, or the perceived shortcomings and handicaps of students and teachers; they focus on schools as institutions that were historically designed and continue to operate in ways that maintain social and economic stratification. There is no such thing as a neutral education process (Freire, 1970). Schools have a sociopolitical purpose of maintaining the status quo by acting as an agent of social control and have only an incidental function of teaching students to solve problems and ask critical questions. As an agent of ideological control, schools preserve their historical purpose—maintaining the existing social order, in which low-income and minority persons are "educated" for less skilled, routine jobs and conditioned by schools for obedience, the acceptance of authority, and external control.

Michael Apple (1983) noted:

Historically social control was a value of educators which was seen as essential to the preservation of the existing social privilege, interests, and knowledge of one element of the population at the expense of less powerful groups. Most often this took the form of attempting to guarantee expert and scientific control in society, to eliminate or socialize unwanted racial or ethnic groups or characteristics or to produce an economically efficient group of citizens in order to reduce the maladjustment of workers to their jobs (p. 86).

If one acknowledges this perspective, it is clear that no matter the method of instruction or the intervention, black children and other minorities will continue to be relegated to the bottom of the status hierarchy. We can reflect on open classrooms, individualized instruction, new math, mastery learning, discovery learning, competency-based learning, activity centers, and remediation and conclude that these strategies have had limited success in enhancing the learning opportunities of minority children.

Many believe that black students' school failure and economic deprivation are related to their inferior intelligence, attributable to blacks' history of slavery, segregation, and limited opportunities. Bowles and Gintis (1983) concluded, however, that although higher IQ and economic success tend to go together, higher IQs are not an important cause of economic success. They found that the intellectual abilities developed and certified in school contribute little to getting ahead economically. The real function of IQ, they contended, is to "legitimate the social institutions underpinning the stratification itself" (p. 242). Schools, in their view, have a mirror relationship with the workplace.

Economic success tends to run in families, and neither schooling nor IQ contributes much to this relationship (Bowles & Gintis, 1983). Additional Census Bureau data confirm that economic success in this country depends on being born into a wealthy family. Twelve percent of American families control 38 percent of household wealth, 63 percent of all stocks, and 52 percent of all bonds and money markets. This disparity has resulted in a $3,397 net worth for black families compared with $32,667 for white families ("Twelve Percent of U.S. Families," 1986). Duncan (cited in Milner, 1972) found that 28 percent of the gap in the occupational status and hence earnings between whites and nonwhites was accounted for by differences in family background and only 20 percent by nonwhites' lower educational achievement.

Milner (1972) reminded us that attempts to narrow this gap between blacks and whites by providing more educational opportunity for blacks are likely to have limited effects. The children of black and white citizens are upwardly mobile in the sense that they will have more education than their parents, simply because average income and the average number of years of formal schooling are increasing. "The crucial question," Milner wrote, "is not whether the sons are better educated than fathers, but whether the sons of poorly educated fathers have less education, wealth, and status than the sons of educated fathers." (p. 43).

Another study that seems to support the notion that IQ and schooling play a less significant role in getting ahead than was previously thought is the work of Schiamberg (1986) of Michigan State. Schiamberg began his study in 1969 with 1,202 impoverished students from the rural South. These students were interviewed again in 1975 and 1979. What Schiamberg discovered was that self-confidence is more important than IQ in determining whether male students get the jobs to which they aspire.

Racism and the devalued position of blacks in our society cannot be ignored as a primary contributing factor to black underachievement. Ogbu (1974) claimed that poor school performance is a defense mechanism, an adaptive behavior that black children use to fend off discrimination. Because black children and their parents saw no possibilities for reaching their goals and ambitions, they simply gave up and failed to take school seriously because school had no relevance to their lives or the lives of significant others. Fordham and Ogbu (1986), in another study, said that children respond positively if they observe that older people in their community usually obtain jobs and other societal benefits commensurate with their schooling.

Eli Ginzberg (1988), in a study sponsored by the National Commission for Employment Policy, corroborated Ogbu's work. In his interviews of eighty Harlem students aged ten to fifteen, a majority of these black youngsters were unable to identify among their relatives, friends, acquaintances a high school graduate who had found the diploma as the way into a good job.

The preponderance of empirical evidence and the existential condition support the credibility of conflict theory. It seems fair to summarize this section by stating that schools operate overtly and covertly to institutionalize the "caste-like" (Ogbu, 1978) status of black children. Instead of existing to expand opportunities for economic success, as the prescriptive view suggests, schools often institutionalize the unequal distribution of resources and serve as an instrument by which the powerful maintain the status quo.

In the following section, the descriptive or institutional context of the model will be discussed by reviewing several school practices that are contradictions to societal prescriptions and beliefs concerning education. The model maintains that these contradictions primarily generate from bias concerning students' race and class. The practices treated in this section include the teaching of the hidden curriculum, tracking, and discriminatory disciplinary practices.

DESCRIPTIVE PRACTICES THAT HARM BLACK CHILDREN

Figure 1.2
Institutional Context

Institutional Context
Descriptive

School Practices and
Policies
1. Curriculum
2. Tracking
3. Disciplinary Practices

Instructional objectives in standard elementary and secondary curriculum guides vary little in relationship to the school's location, social class, race of student body, and even students' ability. One could assume that because mandated courses and instructional objectives are similar, children (no matter their race or class) receive correspondent qualitative and quantitative instruction. This assumption is, of course, unfounded. The stated curriculum does not discriminate, but the hidden, or latent, curriculum does. The hidden curriculum is the unstated but influential knowledge, attitudes, norms, rules, rituals, values, and beliefs that are transmitted to students through structure, policies, processes, formal content, and the social relationships of school. Jackson (1983) has estimated that 90 percent of what transpires in the classroom fits this definition of hidden curriculum.

The following are examples of incidental yet pervasive learning that students absorb early in school:

- Teachers are more powerful than students; principals are more powerful than teachers.
- Some children are called on to perform favors for teachers; others are not.
- Teachers call on well-dressed children more often than poorly dressed children.

- Teachers praise boys more than girls.

- Interruptions and intrusions are frequent and unavoidable.

- No matter how hard some children try to gain the favor and attention of the teacher, some will never succeed.

- Teachers behave more favorably toward the children whose parents participate in school activities.

This hidden curriculum, according to Apple (1983), is not hidden at all, and what this curriculum teaches the majority of black and low-income children is obedience and deference to authority, docility, subordination, extrinsic motivation, external control, dependence, and fatalism. Adoption of these behaviors ultimately predestines black students to low-paying, low-status jobs, diminished self-concepts, and feelings of inferiority.

Jean Anyon and Ray Rist provided illuminating examples of just how the hidden curriculum operates. Anyon (1981) interviewed teachers and principals in four schools in one school district. All the classes were fifth grades, but what she discovered was that although the curriculum objectives were the same for all these children, the hidden curriculum provided drastically different experiences for students of varying social classes.

The students in the executive elite school were instructed in a manner designed to enhance their critical thinking skills. They were taught the value and the processes of independent research, they discussed current issues and social problems, and they were encouraged to give their opinions readily and often. There was much emphasis on how to present oneself publicly and confidently. Teachers accomplished this goal in a number of ways, including elimination of bells that demarcated time and obedient behavior, of lining up, and of controlling the movement of the class. The teachers were never impolite or nasty and seldom shouted direct orders to these children. These students knew they were destined to be the owners and controllers of physical capital and the means of production.

The affluent professional school engaged its students in self-directed and creative work that called for frequent application of ideas, individual thought, and expressiveness. The students produced their own written stories and were asked to independently assess their own competence. Teachers attempted to control the movement of their classes through negotiation in which the students were constantly probed to evaluate the consequences of their misbehavior. Anyon stated that these students were acquiring the symbolic or cultural capital that would prepare them for managerial and professional careers. Symbolic capital includes a strong commitment to hard work and the work ethic, an internal locus of control, and a firm belief in the value of competition.

Middle-class schoolchildren read their daily assignments, pursued the teacher's quest for the one right answer to a question, exercised a limited amount of choice and decision making, and rarely participated in critical thinking or creative endeavors. Their school life was predictable, routine, boring, and uneventful. Their relationship to capital was bureaucratic— rule-bound, lacking in initiative, hierarchical, and inflexible.

The minimum amount of decision making and the maximum amount of rote learning were given to children in the working-class school. The teachers routinely gave the students work with no explanation of its relevance or purpose to life or to previous assignments. Whether or not the work was performed in the sequence the teacher directed was as important as the accuracy of the answer. Seldom were the students asked their opinion, nor did they volunteer. Teachers were neither polite nor tolerant; the primary objective was control. Unlike any of the other schools, there were periods during the day when the children did nothing, a situation that was permissible as long as the children were quiet and subdued.

These working-class schools described by Anyon (1981) reflect the schools that poor black youngsters usually attend. Gouldner (1978) found that teachers in the all-black school in her study thought "a good class had children who had learned to sit quietly at their desks, raise their hands before talking, wait patiently for the bell to ring before leaving their seats, stand in line with their partners in an orderly way, and when in school repress any expression of anger, frustration, or exuberance" (p. 29).

An observation and interview study by Leacock (1969) of one second-grade and one fifth-grade class in four city schools provides an additional perspective on the workings of the hidden curriculum. The four schools represented predominantly low-income white, low-income black, middle-income white, and middle-income black schools.

Hamilton (1983) summarized Leacock's findings:

Middle income schools encouraged students to take initiative and interact with each other through committees and cooperative projects, which were absent in lower income schools, where teacher-student interaction was much more prominent than student-student. Moreover, proper behavior in the lower income schools appeared to be an end in itself rather than the means to establish a climate for learning, which it was in the middle income schools. Teachers in the middle income black school placed much more emphasis on academic learning and were judged to teach more skillfully than teachers in the lower income black school (p. 326).

Perhaps the seminal work on the social relationships of the hidden curriculum is Ray Rist's (1970) work. This longitudinal study of one class of children from kindergarten to second grade is salient because it attests to the relationship between the hidden curriculum and its negative impact on achievement and because the teachers and the students in the observed school were black, suggesting that when the teacher race variable is eliminated, social class becomes a significant variable.

By the eighth day of school, the kindergarten teacher in Rist's study made permanent seating assignments and divided the class into three tables. The children at Table 1 were seated close to her, and there was a high degree of verbal interaction. Rist noted that all these children were well dressed and clean and that the children at the other two tables were poorly dressed, often smelled of urine, and were even darker-skinned. Table 3 students were more likely than Table 1 students to be on welfare and to live in families with six or more children. It became obvious to the children that this kindergarten teacher preferred Table 1 children, perceiving them as "fast learners" and compatible with her prescription of the ideal student. On the other hand, Table 2 and Table 3 students were often ridiculed and treated cruelly by the teacher and eventually by each other.

In the first grade, the new teacher repeated the kindergarten teacher's seating arrangement. That is, no student perceived by the kindergarten teacher as a failure (Tables 2 and 3) was assigned to a fast learners' table in the first grade. The second-grade assignments were no different, leading Rist to describe this classification as a caste phenomenon in which there was absolutely no upward mobility. "No matter how well a child in the lower reading groups might have read, he was destined to remain in the same reading group. That is, in a sense, another manifestation of the self-fulfilling prophecy in that a 'slow learner' had no option but to continue to be a slow learner, regardless of performance or potential" (p. 435).

The hidden curriculum in schools often reinforces society's prejudicial view that black children, particularly low-income black children, are incapable and inferior. In Rist's study, teachers had, by the eighth day of school, already decided that these low-income children could not learn— they were virtually written off as failures at age five! In spite of students' effort, performance, and ability, the teachers in Rist's study ignored data that disconfirmed their stereotypes and prejudices. These descriptions illustrate how schools often collaborate in the maintenance of poverty, inequality, and the unequal status of black people.

Tracking—Educational Ghettos for Black Children

If there is one educational practice that seems to contribute most to the miseducation and nonachievement of black children, it is the practice of placing students in homogenous ability groups. The practice was used in the late nineteenth century as a convenient mechanism both to teach immigrant children who spoke little or no English and to separate these children, whom school officials considered filthy and inferior, from middle-class, American-born students. Unlike the early immigrants from northern Europe, these children of southern and eastern Europe were different not only in language but in religion, traditions, and culture. School officials perceived that their responsibility was to Americanize these foreign students quickly and to make certain that they did not contaminate the native-born, middle-class students.

By World War I, intelligence tests had been developed, and school administrators used these imprecise measures to justify their decisions to separate children (ostensibly by ability but in actuality by class). Lewis Terman, a founding father in the field of testing, wrote in 1916:

> Their dullness seems to be racial, or at least in the family stocks from which they come. The fact that one meets this type with such extraordinary frequency among Indians, Mexicans, and negroes suggests quite forcibly that the whole question of racial differences in mental traits will have to be taken up anew. . . . There will be discovered enormously significant racial differences which cannot be wiped out by any schemes of mental culture. Children of this group should be segregated in special classes. . . . They cannot master abstractions, but they can be made efficient workers (in Oakes, 1985, pp. 36–37).

Today the use of tracking is still widespread and continues to separate children by race and class resulting in the maintenance and reproduction of a system of social and economic stratification. In addition, tracking is an administrative convenience. Students have to be partitioned into smaller instructional groups, and dividing them by ability, on the surface, seems to be sound educational practice. Defenders of the system (Nevi, 1987) claim that it allows for individualized instruction, the development of more positive student self-concepts, and more effective and efficient instruction. But there is overwhelming research evidence that tracking students by ability has no educational benefit for students and in fact is deleterious to academic achievement, extracurricular participation, self-concept, peer relationships, career aspirations, and motivation. Many works support the conclusion that the practice of tracking is indeed curious as little evidence supports its use in school (Goodlad, 1984; Gouldner, 1978; Hallinan & Sorensen, 1983; Lefkowitz, 1972; Metz, 1978; Oakes, 1985; Persell, 1977; Rist, 1973; Rosenbaum, 1976; Rowan & Miracle, 1983). One author (Oakes, 1985) stated, "Homogenous grouping doesn't consistently help anyone learn better" (p. 7).

Tracking begins early in the lives of schoolchildren. Rist's (1970) portrayal of a teacher who made permanent placement assignments by the eighth day of kindergarten is a startling one. It is common practice in elementary schools to assign children to one of three groups—high, average, or low. The children and the faculty know that designations like Cardinals, Robins, and Blue Jays are not simply the names of birds but that they carry with them differential expectations concerning children's achievement, behavior, future success, and home life. The high school curriculum, however, is where tracking is more prevalent and more firmly institutionalized than in elementary school. Students are placed in tracks that produce various diplomas such as vocational, general, academic, or advanced academic. The number of certificates of attendance—statements basically verifying that the students attended school but failed to achieve—is growing. Employers find the vocational diploma of little value in industry and business because the skills taught and the equipment used in high schools tend to be outdated, even obsolete. A study of high school seniors in 1972 concluded that vocational education was least successful for inner-city minority students (Campbell, Gardner, & Seitz, 1982). The general diploma given by the state of Georgia, for instance, does not prepare students to be unconditionally admitted to any of its public four-year state institutions.

How a student gets into a particular track depends on a number of factors. Gilmore (1985) concluded that teachers' perception of black students' attitude was a more important factor than their academic ability for placement in high-track classes. Findley and Bryan (1975), on the other hand, found that 83 percent of school districts nationwide used achievement or IQ tests for placement. The tests provide the guise of objectivity and accountability used to defend the placements. The mere proliferation of these instruments and the profit-making businesses that administer them are also related to the extensive use of standardized tests in educational decision making.

The decision as to the group in which a child belongs is not based on objective criteria alone. It is not uncommon to find that some advanced classes have students in them whose transcripts do not seem to warrant the placement. Rist (1973) found that teachers used apparent signs of middle-class status in making their decisions—dress, language, lack of body odor, and skin color. Persistent parents, mostly middle-class ones, also influence their children's placement. A study using data from *High School and Beyond* (Jones, Van Fossen, & Spade, 1987) concluded that students' social class is strongly related to track placement. The researchers found that two-thirds or more of high-ability, high-SES (socio-economic status) students were in the academic track, but only one-half of the high-ability, low-SES students were enrolled in the academic track. Oakes (1985) and Gouldner (1978) concluded that teachers and counselors have significant latitude in assigning students to classes or groups. Gouldner (1978) wrote the following after interviewing teachers in an all-black inner-city elementary school concerning the criteria used in placement decisions:

> So, as school opened in the fall, the teachers controlled the fates of their young pupils as they went about the business of deciding where to place each child in the stratified order of their classrooms, an order which paralleled their ideas of the world outside. However, they were not necessarily conscious of the criteria they used in making these judgments about their new students. Interviews with teachers probing for information about how they evaluated the pupils were relatively unproductive. Typical were the responses of a teacher who said she believed that some students were "just basically low achievers" and others were "high achievers." Some of the children were "fast learners" and others had "no idea what was going on in the classroom." Whatever the criteria used to evaluate the students' potential, the judgments could only be described as intuitive, since they were not based on objective data (p. 67).

The mere finding that schools assign students to different curricula does not necessarily indicate educational malpractice, nor is the assignment entirely unjustified. Students vary in ability, motivation, persistence, learning style, and numerous other personality traits and behaviors. What is devastating about tracking is that in lower tracks the number of poor and black students is disproportionately high, the instruction is inferior and ineffective, and students suffer psychologically and emotionally.

When tracking is combined with student characteristics of race and class, the result is predictable. Black and poor students are disproportionately enrolled in the lowest ability groups (Eyler, Cook, & Ward, 1982; Metz, 1978; Oakes, 1985; Persell, 1977), a fact that leads to a phenomenon known as resegregation. Resegregation occurs when black students are either intentionally or inadvertently assigned to lower tracks, a practice that results in two schools in one building—one black and one white, "together but unequal" (Welsh, 1986, p. 68). The preponderance of black students in low-ability groups and white children in high-ability groups reinforces beliefs and stereotypes among adults and children that blacks are intellectually inferior to whites.

Welsh (1986), a teacher at prestigious T. C. Williams High School in Alexandria, Virginia, noted that this "Presidential School of Excellence" in reality provides two separate school experiences—a private and superior school experience for white students and a public and inferior school experience for black students. Although the school is evenly divided racially, Welsh noted:

A casual visitor to our school might easily conclude that we are practicing deliberate racial segregation. He'd see mostly whites in the physics lab and mostly blacks in the Career Wing (vocational track). He'd see Phase I (slow track) English classes made up almost entirely of blacks, and advanced English classes with only a few black faces in them. Of the eighty-nine students who took my advanced placement English course for college credit in 1983–84, only seven were black, and five of them tried to drop out—this in a school in which black and white enrollments are almost equal (p. 63).

Meier, Steward, and England (cited in Snider, 1987) analyzed extensive school data from the Office of Civil Rights and the U.S. Census Bureau from 1979 to 1982 regarding factors affecting racial tracking. They concluded that tracking was conscious discrimination to make desegregated school systems more attractive to white parents.

Tracking is undesirable not only because it segregates students but more importantly because the instructional methods used in low-ability groups have been found to be ineffective and to contribute directly to the disruptive behaviors frequently displayed by lower-tracked students. Many of the teachers who are assigned to these lower-tracked groups are often inexperienced, incompetent, or both. Excellent teachers typically have the more advanced classes, and the incompetent ones the low-ability students. Welsh (1986) commented that the teachers in his department avoided teaching the low-track, mostly black classes. An administrator in his school declared: "Given the fact that it's almost impossible to fire horrible teachers, you assign them to the kids whose parents complain the least. That ends up being the lower classes" (p. 66). The incentive system in the profession perpetuates the victimization of black students by rewarding the most competent teachers by assigning these teachers to students who are the least likely to need them.

Brophy (cited in Dusek, 1985) summarized the behaviors of teachers who teach low-track students and the instructional methods that contribute to the further decline of these struggling, low-achieving students:

1. Teachers wait less time for lows to answer.
2. Teachers give lows the answer or call on someone else rather than trying to improve lows' responses by giving clues or repeating or rephrasing the question.
3. Teachers reward inappropriate behavior or incorrect answers by lows.
4. Teachers criticize lows more often for failure.
5. Teachers praise lows less frequently than highs for success.
6. Teachers fail to give feedback to the public responses of lows.
7. Teachers pay less attention to lows or interact with them less frequently.
8. Teachers call on lows less often to respond to questions.
9. Teachers seat lows farther away from themselves.
10. Teachers demand less from lows by teaching them less, by giving less extended explanations and definitions, and by accepting poor quality and often inaccurate responses.
11. Teachers interact with lows more privately than publicly.
12. Teachers grade lows more harshly, giving highs the benefit of the doubt in borderline cases.
13. Teachers are less friendly to lows, smiling less often in interactions with them.
14. Teachers give briefer and less informative feedback to the questions of lows.
15. Teachers provide less direct instruction to lows, giving them more opportunity to practice independently (pp. 309–10).

Allington (1983) found the following in reading instruction:

16. Teachers provide more meaningful discussion of stories with highs.

17. Teachers ask highs more comprehension questions.

18. Teachers allow highs to read silently; lows do more reading aloud (a practice that is negatively correlated to achievement).

Schofield's (1982) ethnographic work in a newly integrated middle school provides a rich description of how homogeneous ability grouping serves as a self-fulfilling prophecy for failure for two black male students, Steve and Brad:

> Steve and Brad, both black, occasionally do Group 1 work, although they are in Group 2. Today at the beginning of class Mr. Hughes says to them, "I want you to work in Group 2 today. They are doing hard work in Group 1. . . ." Mr. Hughes explains the Group 2 problems to the class, saying, "This is very easy to do. I expect you to do it in about 5 minutes." Brad says, "Mr. Hughes, can we do the other problems?" referring to the Group 1 problems. Mr. Hughes replies, "You are going to find them frustrating." It's hard to pick up a clear yes or no in his answer. Brad and Steve watch as he explains the Group 1 problems. Later Mr. Hughes says, "OK, how many people don't know how to do the problems? . . ." Brad raises his hand. Mr. Hughes says to him, "I'm going to have to put you in the other group. These are too hard for you." He goes over to Brad and Steve to get them to work on Group 2 problems. Steve protests, saying, "I'm on number three" (p. 80).

Oakes (1986) found that in high-track secondary English classes, students learned classic and modern fiction, literary genres, narrative writing, and critical thinking. On the other hand, low-track students wrote simple paragraphs, completed worksheets, and practiced filling out job applications. In the mathematics classes, high-track students learned concepts; low-track students practiced computation and memorized math facts. When students are tracked inappropriately, they lose interest, misbehave, and eventually drop out. In a recent national poll (cited in Honig, 1987), 60 percent of black children reported that school was too easy for them.

It is often assumed that the teaching of higher-order thinking skills is appropriate only for high-ability or gifted students; hence, few black students in low tracks are exposed to instruction that emphasizes the higher levels of thinking. In addition, recent national reform reports and state mandates requiring the teaching and assessment of basic skills result in instruction characterized by drill and practice, rote memorization, and teacher-centered activities designed to enhance successful mastery of mandatory competency tests.

Eubanks and Levine (1987) concluded that black students drilled for years in lower-order reading and math skills can now perform fairly well on standardized tests through the sixth or seventh grades. Unfortunately, "many can only call out the words without understanding what they read, or are able to do simple arithmetic operations without understanding the math concepts or problem-solving methods required for success in school or in a modern economy" (p. 25).

Why is the teaching of higher-level, critical thinking skills important? Is the teaching of these skills particularly crucial for black students? Combs (1979) states that schools are preparing students for a world that does not exist in the present and certainly not in the future. Because information and knowledge emerge and expand at unimaginable rates, the tedious practice of drilling, repeating, and memorizing facts is indeed obsolete. One-half of the information in a particular field becomes out-dated in six years (McTighe & Schollenberger, 1985); by 1990, information will double every twenty minutes (Beyer, 1987). The constant search for the most appropriate fact-oriented, content-specific curriculum in a shrinking, complex, incredibly changing world is a futile and frustrating effort. The skills necessary for survival in the twenty-first century should include problem solving, creativity, and, above all, the capacity to be introspective, self-directed, adaptive, open-minded, and tolerant of change and ambiguity. Combs (1979) writes, "In the world of tomorrow, a bigot may be far more dangerous than a bad reader" (p. 81).

Black and other low-income minority students constantly face situations in their surroundings that require critical thinking skills. The ghettos and barrios are threatening environments, where survival depends on such critical instincts as the ability to solve problems, analyze, ask relevant questions, and make immediate and astute observations. Even when minority students do not live in ghettos and barrios, they need training in critical thinking skills to respond to overt and subtle racist behaviors they are likely to encounter. Blacks' physical and emotional well-being depends on the ability to judge credible sources, look for alternatives and evidence, detect bias, distinguish between facts and opinions, understand contradictions of words and behaviors, and analyze the unstated as well as the stated.

Finally, tracking affects students' self-concepts, their relationships with peers and teachers, and their career aspirations. Oakes (1985) and Persell (1977) found that low-track students felt alienated, inferior, excluded, and negative about themselves. Their interactions with their peers were con-

frontational and accompanied by frequent outbursts of yelling and fighting, unlike high-track students, who were competitive, yet helpful and
friendly to each another. The relationships between teachers and students
were negative for low-track students and positive for high-track students.
Low-track students thought that teachers were punitive and lacked concern
for them; high-track students did not feel this way.

What makes this system so pernicious is the fact that once assigned to
a track, students seldom move either up or down. Rosenbaum (1976)
compared the system of tracking to a tournament: "When you win, you
win only the right to go on to the next round; when you lose, you lose
forever" (p. 40). He found that movement from one track to another was
rare and that when students did move, they were seven times more likely
to move downward than upward. The label of low- or high-achiever is
affixed in elementary school, follows the student through the middle years,
and becomes a self-fulfilling prophecy by high school. Few schools use
organizational structures that accommodate students who are above
average in one subject and below average in another. These inflexible and
unyielding placements assume that one's intelligence is measurable,
unidimensional, fixed, and unalterable and that achievement is general,
not specific to a subject.

Black students are particularly injured by this practice because their race
and class are associated with low achievement. Once placed in the low
tracks, they are taught less effectively, they interact hostilely with teachers
and peers, and they develop negative self-esteem, and all of these results
lead to a vicious cycle of school failure and antisocial behaviors. Indeed,
black students must take responsibility for their behaviors and attitudes
that lead to nonachievement, but the educational profession must bear the
responsibility for its failure to provide an equal educational opportunity.

Disciplinary Practices

One factor related to the nonachievement of black students is the
disproportionate use of severe disciplinary practices, which leads to black
students' exclusion from classes, their perceptions of mistreatment, and
feelings of alienation and rejection, which result ultimately in their misbehaving more and/or leaving school. According to data (Carnegie Corporation of New York, 1984/1985; Eyler, Cook, and Ward, 1982), black
students, compared to whites, are two to five times as likely to be
suspended at a younger age. In addition, black students are more likely to
receive lengthier repeated supensions. This same Carnegie study reported
that although minority students represent 25 percent of the nationwide

school population, they constituted 40 percent of all suspended and expelled students. In Kentucky, for instance, black students made up 12 percent of the 1980 school enrollment but 31 percent of the school suspensions. They were, in addition, more likely to receive corporal punishment.

Taylor and Foster (1986) gathered and analyzed school suspension records for one school district in the Southeast for the academic year 1983–1984. The data included ten elementary schools, five junior high schools, and four high schools. Although black students composed 54 percent of the enrollment, they represented 67 percent of the students suspended at all levels of schooling. The educational implications are dramatic. Black males in this one district during one academic year missed 159 days of school, in comparison with 62 days for white males, 32 days for black females, and 4 days for white females.

Many educators speculate that low-income black children bring to school a set of antischool behaviors and traits that emanate from a culture of poverty. They rationalize their harsh treatment of these children by citing instances of an undisciplined and unstructured home life, a lack of positive male models, an early exposure to crime and delinquency, and a disrespect for adult authority figures. This victimization approach ignores other important factors such as teachers' stereotypes; attitudes about race, class, and gender; and the degree of teacher subjectivity in dispensing punishment unequally.

Stereotyping occurs when teachers perceive black students, particularly black males, by virtue of their race, sex, and class, to be potential sources of classroom disruptions. Media portrayals of black people have depicted black youth as violent, gang-oriented, and abusive. Researchers have found that these stereotypes do exist in the schools. Gottlieb (1964) found that white teachers believed that black students were aggressive, unindustrious, hostile, and rebellious. Woolridge and Richman (1985) found that their sample of 216 southern teachers was less likely than their white male peers to punish black males, and these researchers concluded that the teachers' reluctance to do so was associated with a belief that because black students fight and steal anyway, punishment would be a waste of the teachers' time and energy. When teachers did punish black students, they punished black males and black females with similar, severe forms of discipline. However, sharp distinctions were made between white males and white females; white females received milder punishments, an indication of their preferred status.

Discrimination in disciplinary practices occurs because there are no absolute definitions of disorderly behavior. According to Stebbins (1970), a teacher's reaction to disruption is based not solely on the behavior but on the identification of the student who violated the classroom rules. Teachers consider the students' past deportment, social class, and academic achievement when they determine the punishment appropriate for a transgression. High achievers are not punished as severely as low achievers for the same infraction. When a black student is identified as the student who misbehaved, it seems quite possible that the transgression is evaluated with reference not only to the individual child, but to the race, sex, and class groups to which the student belongs. For black males, the outcome can be alarmingly discriminatory.

Eyler, Cook, and Ward (1982) reported that black students in desegregated schools were suspended for subjective rather than objective offenses. Subjective offenses reflect a teacher's personal judgment. Such offenses include disobedience, insubordination, disrespectful behavior, and dress code violations. White students were suspended for more objective offenses such as drugs, assault, truancy, and the possession of alcohol or drugs. A study by the National Coalition of Advocates for Students (NCAS, 1987) supported the research by Eyler and her colleagues. The NCAS work revealed that black students are suspended not because they commit serious offenses, but because they do not get along with a particular teacher. The research emphasized that the problem is that teachers tend to overreact to the behavior of black students, particularly black male students.

In a study by Gouldner (1978), 242 black inner-city elementary classrooms were observed throughout a school year. Gouldner heard many kindergarten and first-grade teachers complain about the black students' belligerent and disruptive behavior. She was prepared to see instances of abusive behavior—hitting, pulling, throwing, defiance, and loud talking. When Gouldner and her colleagues observed the classrooms, however, they rarely saw the children misbehave in ways that matched the teachers' prior descriptions. Instead, the researchers saw children getting out of their seats, wandering around the room, opening drawers, rattling papers, leaning across the table, talking with other children, calling out to get the teacher's attention, and turning toward or touching another child. These minor student disruptions, which were associated with the teachers' lack of management skills, occurred when students were unoccupied, when they made transitions to other periods, and when they became bored with drawn-out recitation sessions; they did not occur because the children were uncontrollable, incapable, or unwilling to learn.

An ethnographic study of two deviant kindergarten boys, one black and one white, revealed differential teacher treatment for identical behavior

(Emihovich, 1983). The teacher was indulgent of the misbehavior of the white male, interpreting his deviant behavior as that of a bright, bored child whom she had failed as a teacher. On the other hand, the black male child was viewed as pathological and deviant. Emihovich's (1983) findings support the work of Woolridge and Richman (1985) in that the teacher enforced stricter controls on the white boy's behavior, which had beneficial effects for that student. In contrast, the black child was not provided these teacher-imposed controls, a fact that suggests the notion that disciplining the black child would not make a difference.

In summary, discriminatory disciplinary practices damage black students' educational progress and life chances. Uneven dispensations of punishment by teachers cause more student misbehavior. When students do not attend school regularly, they eventually fail. If the student perceives his race to be a factor, the results are feelings of alienation, hostility, conflict, and often aggression on the part of the student.

The school practices described in this section contribute to strained interpersonal relationships, hidden conflict, and lack of cultural synchronization, which is described in the following chapter.

2

Cultural Synchronization

Mrs. Jones, the teacher, passes out some dittos to her eighth-grade students. One young man, Cedric, shouts to her, "Mrs. Jones, ain't got nam!"

She frowns and says, "What?" The children snicker.

Cedric mumbles, "Forget it."

A young female says to the teacher, "Ms. Jones, I need annurder one. This one tore up."

The teacher shouts, "What? I can't hear you."

Cedric interjects sarcastically, "Ms. Jones deef." Everyone laughs. Mrs. Jones stands in amazement, confused and frustrated. The lesson begins, and Mrs. Jones lectures while joyless, bored students sit passively. Only three of the twenty students appear to be listening. The lesson deteriorates rapidly.

Figure 2.1
Interpersonal Context

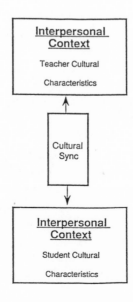

Cedric puts his head down on the desk and begins to fall asleep. Mrs. Jones shouts, "Wake up, Cedric, or you will be in trouble."

The student lifts his head slowly, stares angrily at the teacher and says, "What she be tripping about now?"

Mrs. Jones shouts, "What did you say?" The children laugh aloud. Mrs. Jones demands, "Cedric, get your textbook out and turn to today's lesson." Cedric reaches under the desk and fumbles with the many loose papers in his bookbag. Two minutes pass, and Cedric is still pretending to look for his work. Mrs. Jones interrupts the lesson again and warns Cedric, "If your work is not on your desk in the next minute, you'll be seeing me in detention hall." Cedric smiles, and Mrs. Jones grabs Cedric's new leather bookbag and throws it on the floor. "See me after class."

"Don't be putting my bag on the floor," the student shouts. "It brand new."

"I don't care," says Mrs. Jones. Cedric puts his head on his desk and stares out the window. A tired, dejected, and despondent Mrs. Jones goes home and decides to call Cedric's grandmother, his legal guardian. She carefully relays the day's events. She tells the grandmother, "Mrs. Washington, Cedric's negative attitude and lack of enthusiasm for school are preventing him from actively participating in the instructional activities. I'm afraid that he might be retained next year if he does not show dramatic improvement in these areas."

The grandmother hesitates and says, "Thank you for calling, and I'm gonna get that boy when he gets in here. Didn't I tell y'all that it's O.K. to beat him. That's what I have to do."

Mrs. Jones ends the conversation with Cedric's grandmother and confirms the notions that Cedric is incorrigible and that the grandmother is uninterested and certainly abusive.

What this episode illustrates is cultures in conflict. Mrs. Jones is a well-intentioned teacher who wants desperately for her students to learn. However, she does not understand their culture-language, values, home environment, or learning styles.

Culture, according to Ogbu (1988b), is a way of life shared by members of a population. It includes shared knowledge, customs, emotions, rituals, traditions, values, and norms that are embodied in a set of behaviors designed for survival in a particular environment.

Research by Byers and Byers (1972) has provided some help in understanding the cultural and racial implications of synchronization between teacher and student. Byers and Byers investigated the nonverbal communication between teachers and students by filming the interaction between a white teacher and two black and two white girls in nursery school. They found that one of the white girls was more active and successful in getting the teacher's attention. She looked at the teacher fourteen times, and the teacher reciprocated eight of these times. On the other hand, the more initiating black girl looked at the teacher thirty-five times but caught the teacher's eye only four times. The researchers concluded that the black girl, unlike her white counterpart, timed her glances inappropriately and made inappropriate moves at crucial times, pulling when she should have pushed or pushing when she should have pulled. The black girl, unlike the white girl, did not share with the teacher an implicit understanding of cultural nuances, gestures, and timing, a lack that resulted in frustration and missed learning opportunities for the black child. On the other hand, the white girl's shared cultural and racial identity produced many instances of expressed affection and learning opportunities.

Heath (1983) described differences in questioning behaviors of white and black children at home and at school. White middle-class parents and white middle-class teachers used "known-answer" questions, which solicited responses to names, shapes, and colors of objects. On the other hand, the black children and their parents engaged in more sophisticated verbal storytelling involving the uses of metaphors and analogies. In school, black children asked questions such as "What's that like?" or "Who's he acting like?" rather than the more middle-class attributional "What's that?" The teachers in the study failed to recognize or take advantage of the more developed questioning styles of the black children. Instead they emphasized and rewarded the white children's questioning behaviors, leaving the black children perplexed and probably bored.

These incidents are explicit examples of what occurs in schools when teachers and students lack correspondence or are not synchronized because of differences in culture. The white teacher and the white child understood the unstated rules and the subtleties of the majority culture's verbal and nonverbal communicative processes. For the white child, interaction and learning with the teacher were productive and enjoyable; the black child had the opposite experience.

The concept of cultural synchronization is based on anthropological and historical research that advances the finding that black Americans have a distinct culture founded on identifiable norms, language, behaviors, and attitudes from Africa. M. J. Herskovits (1958) was one of the first to identify these African retentions, such as funeral practices, songs, dances, dress, religious practices, beliefs in magic and the occult, and the concept of time. His work countered the prevailing myth that black people lacked a culture of their own and that little or no African retentions had survived the trans-Atlantic crossing and the institution of slavery. Blacks were patronizingly considered only poor imitators of European culture and genetically, psychologically, and culturally inferior to whites.

Present-day manifestations of Africanisms, researchers claim, are most prevalent in lower-class black communities where racial isolation persists and assimilation into the majority culture is minimal. These blacks have been called ordinary, common, average, typical (Pasteur & Toldson, 1982), and community blacks (Kochman, 1981), and although there are regional, social class, and gender variations in the displayed behaviors, there seems to be what Boykin (1986) calls a distinctive cultural deep structure, which reflects a pattern of attributes and exhibitions. Ogbu (1988a) believes that urban and suburban blacks share a distinct social identity, a sense of peoplehood, and a distinct cultural frame of reference. Banks (1988), countering William Wilson's (1978) assertion that class, not race, determines the life chances of Afro-Americans, concluded that even though blacks may be considered middle-class, their ethnicity influences their behavior. He discussed the variable called generational middle-class status; that is, blacks who are first-generation middle-class are very different from whites who have been middle-class for several generations. Middle-class blacks tend to be very intimate with lower-class relatives and attend activities with lower-class blacks such as churches and clubs. Hence, some of these cultural characteristics are often found in both black middle and lower classes, as well as in black Canadian and British communities (Solomon, 1988).

Current data support the supposition that not only do blacks have a culture that is distinct, African-based, identifiable, and more ancient than European culture but that the two cultures are incongruous and contradictory. Boykin (1986) made the comparisons in Table 2.1.

Recent scholars, including Boykin (1986), Hilliard (1983), Kochman (1981), and Pasteur and Toldson (1982), have described the idiosyncratic nature of Afro-American cultural life. Boykin (1986) described the "triple quandary" of black Americans by stating that they operate simultaneously in three realms—the African-based black culture, the mainstream Eurocentric culture, and the oppressed minority. Boykin (1986) summarized the works of several scholars and concluded that black cultures contain at least nine interrelated dimensions (p. 61): (1) Spirituality—an approach in which life is viewed as vitalistic rather than mechanistic; (2) harmony—the idea that humans and nature live interdependently and in harmony; (3) movement—an emphasis on rhythm, music, and dance; (4) verve—a propensity for relatively high levels of stimulation; (5) affect—an emphasis on emotions and feelings; (6) communalism—a commitment to social connectedness and an awareness that responsibilities to the group transcend individual privileges; (7) expressive individualism—a value on genuine personal expression; (8) oral tradition—a preference for oral/aural communication with a value on spoken language that uses alliterations, metaphors, and colorful forms (see Heath's 1982 study); and (9) and social time perspective—an orientation to time as social rather than material space.

Table 2.1
Comparison of African and European Cultures

African	European
Spiritualism	Materialism
Harmony with nature	Mastery over nature
Organic metaphor	Mechanistic metaphors
Expressive movement	Impulse control
Interconnectedness	Separateness
Affect	Reason
Event orientation	Clock orientation
Orally based culture	Print-based culture
Expressive individualism	Possessive individualism
Uniqueness valued	Sameness valued
Person-to-person orientation	Person-to-person orientation

Source: Boykin, 1986, p. 63.

Rhythm is the essential word that Pasteur and Toldson (1982) used to characterize black culture. They referred to this concept as the "basic ingredient of black expressiveness" (p. 63). Rhythm is closely related to Boykin's spirituality, harmony, movement, verve, affect, and expressive individualism. Pasteur and Toldson (1982) outlined five aspects that further define rhythm and black expressiveness. First, depth of feeling is evidenced by black children's highly charged, noisy, and emotional expressions. The second aspect—naturalistic attitudes—refers to blacks' aversion to formality, their frankness of manner, their casualness in social transaction, their contempt for artificiality, and their acceptance, without guilt or shame, of their sensuality and sexuality. Style—the third characteristic—is the manner in which blacks present and display their uniqueness. Fourth is the poetic and prosaic vernacular, in which peculiarly black speech rhythms, voice inflections, and tonal patterns are used. Finally, expressive movement is the heavy dependence on dance and music in everyday activities.

Hanna (1988) provides a pointed school example:

> Most black children carried themselves differently: More swagger, looseness, swing, hand rapping, "appropriate" dress, "right talk," and sparring characterized their activities. The polyrhythmic walk of many blacks exuded dynamism as parts of the torso moved counter to each other; hips shifted or rotated sideways while the upper torso was held relatively upright. Boys often walked with a springiness, the heel only momentarily placed on the ground. . . . When children were asked to line up, black boys more commonly than white boys would swing on a nearby pole or sprawl on a nearby table (p. 68).

Cultural misunderstandings between teachers and students result in conflict, distrust, hostility, and possible school failure for black students. The conflict is exaggerated because of cultural inversion and cultural aversion. Cultural inversion is related to black students' perceptions that certain behaviors are characteristic of white Americans and hence inappropriate for blacks. Ogbu (1988b) maintained that black students do not feel that the cultural differences they encounter are obstacles that need to be overcome. He said, "Rather, involuntary minorities see these cultural differences as symbols of identity to be maintained" (p. 24). Therefore, some black students do not speak standard English or study in school because these behaviors are thought to be "white-like" and might jeopardize their identity and status with peer group members.

Cultural aversion is the reluctance of teachers and administrators to discuss race and race-related issues like ethnicity, culture, prejudice, equality, and social justice. This color-blind philosophy is linked to educators' uncomfortableness in discussing race, their lack of knowledge of the cultural heritage of their students and the students' peers, and their fears and anxieties that open consideration of differences might incite racial discord or perhaps upset a fragile, often unpredictable, racial harmony. Schofield's (1982) and Fine's (1988) research illustrates how teachers avoided any references to children's racial membership, pretending not to notice that their students came from different ethnic groups, social classes, and cultures.

Lack of synchronization increases, not decreases, when teachers and administrators pretend that they don't notice students' racial membership. One principal in Schofield's (1982) research said: "I really don't address myself to group differences when I am dealing with youngsters. . . . I try to treat youngsters as youngsters and not as black, white, green, or yellow. . . . Children are children" (p. 30). Although this educator is correct that children are more alike than different, the color-blind approach denies the legitimacy of students' heritage and race and often contributes to a cycle of misunderstanding that leads to unstated and unvented hostility between teachers and students, which often results in more misunderstanding and confrontations.

Three cultural characteristics are particularly problematic for black children in school settings because they are largely incompatible with the white middle-class school norms. These three characteristics are (a) style, or manner of personal presentation; (b) use of black English; and (c) cognition, or the processes of knowing and perceiving.

STYLE

The language, style of walking, glances, and dress of black children, particularly males, have engendered fear, apprehension, and overreaction among many teachers and school administrators. The fear and trepidation that black youngsters are able to engender in adults have contributed to the exaggeration and continued use of these behaviors. Cooke (1972) provided interesting photographs of black nonverbal communicative styles, such as giving or getting skin (hand greetings), standing stances, and walking stances.

The verbal communication style of black students baffles school personnel, especially white teachers, who fail to understand black students' expressive language. Verbal ability is valued as highly as physical ability among black males. Foster (1974) included many illustrations of black verbal encounters in his book *Ribbin', Jivin', and Playin' the Dozens*. He stated that whenever black males, young and old, assemble, a boasting or teasing encounter usually ensues. The contest of words is an important male ritual in the black community. Smitherman (cited in Pasteur & Toldson, 1982) described the talking styles as "exaggerated language; mimicry; proverbial statement and aphoristic phrasing; punning and plays on words; spontaneity and improvisation; image-making and metaphor; braggadocio; indirection; and total semantics" (p. 191). Students call these verbal communications by a variety of names—ribbing, jiving, woofing, signifying, playing the dozens, capping, joning, styling, profiling.

For young black males, this verbal sparring often turns into rough-and-tumble play. Schofield (1982) made note of this play in her work and speculated that this activity among black males intimidated and threatened the white children, who often misinterpreted playful acts as attacks. She described a vicious cycle where "whites ignored or withdrew from blacks because of fear of their rough-and-tumble style. Blacks interpreted whites' behavior as motivated by prejudice or conceit and, being angered by such treatment, engaged in more clearly aggressive behavior, which frightened whites even more" (p. 121).

A typical display of nonverbal defiance is "stylized sulking." Gilmore (1985) stated:

> Girls will frequently pose with their chins up, closing their eyelids for long periods and casting downward side glances. . . . A girl also will rest her chin on her hand with her elbow supported by the desk. . . . Striking or getting into pose is usually performed with an abrupt movement or a verbal marker like "humpf." . . . [Boys'] stylized sulking is usually characterized by head downward, arms crossed at the chest, legs spread wide, and desk pushed away (p. 117).

Black students' style of dressing has invoked many mandatory school dress codes. Their dress has been characterized as conspicuous, colorful, visually stimulating, expressive, and intense (Kochman, 1981; Toldson & Pasteur, 1982). Kochman claimed that black males and females, more than whites, associate clothing with self-worth. Unfortunately, designer hats, sunglasses, jeans, athletic shoes, and gold jewelry are status symbols that black teens use to express their self-worth in a world that consistently sends messages about their powerlessness and inferiority. Interestingly, as majority-status teens adopt black cultural dress styles, schools become more tolerant and less punitive.

Kochman (1981), in the book *Black and White Styles in Conflict*, stated:

> Blacks and whites assume they are operating according to identical speech and cultural conventions and that these are the conventions the socially dominant white group has established as standard. This assumption—besides adding to the disruptive capacity of cultural differences—speaks to the general public failure to recognize that black norms and conventions in these areas differ from those of whites (p. 8).

Kochman (1981) and Hanna (1988) provided more specifics of how the differences in black and white cultural styles interfere significantly in the communications and learning processes. They made the following general observations about modal black and white behaviors:

1. Blacks' behavior tends often to be high-key, animated, interpersonal, confrontational, intense, dynamic, and demonstrative. Whites tend often to be low-key, dispassionate, impersonal, nonchallenging, and emotionally restrained. When black students present their ideas in this high-energy style, teachers consider them lacking in self-control and aggressive.

2. Blacks often make distinctions between an argument used to debate difference of opinion and an argument used to ventilate anger and hostility. When whites debate a difference of opinion, they often use discussion that lacks affect and confrontation. Many black students are punished for "fighting" when they are simply arguing to vent their anger. For whites, fighting is a verbal as well as a physical confrontation. Blacks consider fighting physical provocation only.

3. Blacks advocate the material they present in a discussion, relying on their personal experiences. Whites often relate to materials as spokespersons, as if ideas had an objective, not an emotional, dimension.

4. Blacks do not believe that a person has a right to refuse to communicate. Whites do. Black students are often suspicious of whites who "have no opinion" or are unresponsive concerning matters of importance to them. Common refrains in black children's speech include "Do you know what I mean?" and "I know that's right." These solicitous remarks are black students' attempts to involve and engage others in the conversation.

5. Blacks more readily question the authority of knowledge or ideas that have been published or certified by experts. Whites are more likely to regard as authoritative anything attested by experts. When black students interject their personal viewpoints and question the findings of published authors, teachers infer that blacks are illogical, unintelligent, and naive.

6. In a heated discussion, blacks frequently make their points whenever they can enter the discussion. Deference is given to the person who considers his or her point most urgent. Turn-taking is the style of whites, who usually raise their hands to be recognized. Teachers find black students impolite, aggressive, and boisterous when they cut off another student or fail to restrain themselves so that every student can have a turn to talk.

7. Blacks hesitate to share information about their personal lives. Whites often begin their conversations with queries concerning one's occupation, place of residence, number of children, birthplace. Black students often become hostile and recalcitrant when teachers and administrators ask questions that black students consider intrusive and improper.

8. Black students may not maintain constant eye contact with teachers as do white students. Often black children are accused of not paying attention when they are.

9. Black students are more likely than white students to challenge or test school personnel because of beliefs that leadership is derived not from position, credentials, or experience but through personal attributes of strength, forcefulness, persuasiveness, and generosity.

LANGUAGE

The issue of black students' language in school is a critical variable because school success is largely dependent on competent usage of the language. Like race, language is an obvious characteristic and becomes a method that teachers use to separate and stereotype. Black students who speak standard English are perceived to be of higher ability and more middle-class than black students who speak black English. Lightfoot (1978), on this point, stated that the language of black children is symbolic of social and cultural deviance and becomes the basis of teachers' hostility toward black children.

When black students use a more informal, nonstylistic manner of verbal communication, they are likely to speak black English. School personnel consider this language an inferior dialect or a variant of standard English. Researchers (Dillard, 1977; Smitherman, 1977; Williamson, 1975) have concluded that black English is a highly structured, well-formed grammatical system that includes many forms similar in grammar and structure to languages found in West Africa (Baratz & Baratz, 1972; Smitherman, 1977). Labov (1970, 1972) posited that black English has its own distinct logic, grammatical coherence, and system of rules.

Because black students' spoken language does not match the requirements of standard written language, successful black students must learn code switching, translating into standard English before they write or speak.

The greatest differences between black English and standard English are in grammatical structure. Smitherman (1977) attributed these differences to the fact that grammar is the most rigid and fixed aspect of speech, least likely to change over time. Thus, the grammatical patterns of black English have been the last component of the dialect to change.

Some of the most consistent patterns of black English (Baron, 1975; Dillard, 1977; Smitherman, 1977; Williamson, 1975) include the omission of the verb *to be*; *ed* from past tense or past participle construction; *s* or *'s* to indicate plurality or possession; and the articles *a*, *an*, and *the*. Black English verb forms often do not distinguish between singular and plural forms. It is common to hear some black children say, "She have my books." Another frequent characteristic is the plural forms of words, like *childrens, womens, mens*, or *peoples*.

It is not to be inferred that all black people speak black English or that all black-English speakers use these patterns at all times. This description of black language structural patterns is an attempt to bridge both a linguistic and a cultural gap between black English and standard English in order to facilitate communication in the school. In addition, it is hoped that these analyses will encourage further research into the merits of bidialectalism, by which we may discover and nurture hundreds of otherwise talented minority students who are stigmatized because they have not sufficiently mastered standard English. Eleanor Wilson Orr's (1987) research is an example of this effort.

COGNITION

The influential work of Jean Piaget asserts that children's thinking progresses in four stages: sensorimotor, preoperations, concrete operations, and formal operations. Anthropologists questioned the universality of Piaget's theory after discovering that the cognitive styles of many non-Western children do not conform to the model (Lubeck, 1985).

It is often believed that black and white children in Western culture perceive the world and process and organize information differently (Anderson, 1988; Hilliard, cited in Hale-Benson, 1986; Pasteur & Toldson, 1982; Shade, 1982) and that these differences negatively affect black students' achievement. Hilliard (cited in Hale-Benson, 1986) posited that schools approach curriculum and instruction from an analytical rather than a relational cognitive style. Black students are assumed to be relational, that is, predisposed to learning characterized by freedom of movement, variation, creativity, divergent thinking approaches, inductive reasoning, and a focus on people. Schools, on the other hand, emphasize the analytical style, that is, learning characterized by rules and restriction of movement, standardization, conformity, convergent thinking approaches, deductive reasoning, and a focus on things.

Peters (1981) summarized the predicament of black children: when the black lower-class child goes to school at age four or five, he or she discovers that the behavioral rules have now changed. While there are attractive "things" to explore, there is also a new emphasis on sitting still. Play and interaction with others are encouraged only during specific times of day. Music is heard only at "music time." Physical activity, body movement, and expression, not being associated with cognitive learning, are relegated to "activity" or play periods or "physical education." The child is often lost, punished, or put down in the process (p. 84).

Pasteur and Toldson (1982) even hypothesized that blacks and whites are governed by different hemispheres of the brain. Blacks are thought to be dominated by the right hemisphere—intuitive, nonverbal, creative, artistic, spontaneous, and expressive. The left-brain orientation, assumed to be the dominant hemisphere for whites, is logical, mathematical, sequential, and characterized by thought discrimination, and separateness. Although this analysis seems somewhat simplistic (Levy, 1983), black children do seem to use information-processing and cognitive strategies that are culturally specific.

In the most comprehensive review of the literature on Afro-American cognitive styles, Shade (1982) concluded that more research is needed before definitive statements can be proposed. However, Shade contended that "there does appear to be a racial difference in each of the dimensions subsumed under the cognitive style construct" (p. 226). The differences she found in social cognition include the findings that blacks' recognition patterns focus on affective rather than physical characteristics and that black children prefer a variety of stimuli in the learning environment and a variety of teaching methods and materials. As for perceptual style, Shade concluded that blacks have a field-dependent rather than a field-independent cognitive style. Field-dependent individuals have a more global and interrelated approach to visual information and are thus unable to distinguish the necessary parts for problem solving. The opposite approach, field independence, is characteristic of persons who are able to isolate the necessary parts from distracting elements in order to solve problems. Finally, Shade found that blacks' categorizing behavior is more oriented toward the theme and function than toward the specific attributes of the objects categorized. Heath (1982) found evidence of this behavior in the questioning style of black parents.

This treatment of cultural differences does not imply a superiority or inferiority relationship between Eurocentric (analytical) and Afrocentric (relational) styles. Unfortunately, most teachers use one method of instruction, analytical, and ignore relational methods, hence they fail to capitalize on the strengths of black and other children's learning modalities, directly contributing to these students' school failure. In addition, because black students have generally not been taught by a variety of methods and with a variety of materials that are compatible with different cognitive styles, accusations of inferiority and lack of motivation are premature and unwarranted. This author recognizes that some advocates of minority children fear that any acknowledgment of cultural differences results in more negative racial stereotyping, differential treatment, and teacher expectations. On the other hand, attention to these cultural differences in the organization and delivery of instruction appears to be relevant for minority students' success (Au, 1980; Heath, 1983).

DESEGREGATION AND DISAPPEARING BLACK EDUCATORS: FACTORS RELATED TO AN INCREASING LACK OF SYNCHRONIZATION

The lack of cultural correspondence between black children and their teachers relates directly to the declining numbers of black teachers and black principals in public schools. As noted in the review of the literature in Chapter 3, the race of the teacher of black children does make a difference because white teachers seem to have more negative expectations and perceptions and fewer personal relationships with black students than black teachers have.

There has been a serious decline in the number of minority, particularly black, teachers. Predictions for the year 1990 indicate that minority teachers will compose 5 percent of the teaching force, significantly less than the 12 percent of 1980 (J.P. Smith, 1988). This decline in the numbers of black teachers and school administrators in public schools is an issue that has generated much concern among educators and their professional organizations, such as the Carnegie Forum on Education, NEA (National Education Association), AFT (American Federation of Teachers), and the newly created Holmes Group. In 1985, the board of directors of NEA passed the following resolution:

The NEA believes that multiracial teaching staffs are essential to the operation of nonsegregated schools. The Association deplores the current trend of diminishing numbers of minority educators. The

Association urges local and state affiliates and appropriate governing bodies and agencies to work to increase the number of minority teachers and administrators to a percentage at least equal to, but not limited to, the percentage of the minority in the general population (Futrell & Robinson, 1986, pp. 100–101).

The downturn has been so drastic that some authors (Cole, 1986; Edwards, 1981; Rodman, 1985) have referred to black teachers and principals as "endangered species," a reference that has led to speculations and fears that in the near future black and white children might be "confronted with exclusively white authority figures" ("Carnegie Forum on Education," 1986, p. 32).

In this country, teaching has historically attracted a disproportionate number of poor and minority persons who entered the profession as a vehicle for upper mobility. This statement is particularly true for black female college graduates. It has been estimated that in 1950 one-half of all black professionals in the United States were teachers (Cole, 1986) and that 68.8 percent of these black teachers were trained in southern, historically black institutions (Trent, 1984). Teaching, nursing, and social work provided stable, secure, sex-typed job opportunities for black women, and such positions have been accorded prestige and status in the black community. As long as black children remained segregated by law and custom from white children, teaching continued to be a viable, sometimes the only, career opportunity available.

Desegregation

Desegregation dramatically changed the existing social order. Previously semiautonomous black schools became controlled and dominated by white administrators who generally ignored the educational matters of black schools. Sowell (1976) described the relationship between black schools and the white power structure. He stated that under the dual school system in the era of racial segregation, the lack of interest in black schools by all-white boards of education allowed wide latitude to black subordinates to run the "black part" of the system, as long as no problems became visible. The 1954 Brown decision dictated that white school boards and superintendents be in control of critical personnel decisions, such as hiring, firing, and transferring, in previously all-black schools.

The personnel decisions resulted in the firing and transferring of many black teachers after desegregation. Ethridge (1979) estimated that between 1954 and 1972 at least 39,386 black teachers lost their jobs in seventeen southern states. These numbers do not reflect the vast numbers of the black community's most competent teachers who were reassigned to schools in the white community, a prevalent practice then and now.

The desegregation movement has significantly contributed to cultural discontinuity between black students and their schools. Specifically, black people perceived that they had lost control over their vital institutional structures, no longer autonomous and independent from external forces (Irvine & Irvine, 1983). The segregated black community was in some sense an imposed condition. The important point, however, is that this imposed circumstance turned into a functional system. The boundaries became demarcated, and the segregated black community acted as a protective mechanism to screen out the harmful effects of racial diatribes hurled at its members from the larger, hostile society. It had governing and regulating norms; it constrained and sanctioned its members.

The black church stood at the center of black institutional life, free from white control and white domination. It alone could claim complete independence and autonomy. Second in importance to the lives of blacks were their schools. Black schools were semiautonomous organizations and were, for all intents and purposes, controlled by blacks, in the sense that they were administered by black principals, staffed by black teachers, and served a black student population. More significant to the issue of independence is the fact that these schools represented and took on uniquely stylized characteristics reflective of its members—patterns of communication, cultural preferences, and normatively diffused modes of behavior.

Black schools during the segregation era were extremely complex organizations. They were not only educational institutions in the ordinary sense of that term but institutions that addressed the deeper psychological and sociological needs of their clients. Sowell (1976), citing an interview with a black principal in New Orleans, described the principal's experiences in an all-black school—recollections of how teachers promoted the idea of the worth of the individual and how they always called the boys "Mister" and the girls "Miss," emotionally important titles denied even adult blacks throughout the South at the time.

Still, at other levels, these schools solidified the communities they served. They provided clothing for needy children. These schools were the centerpiece of community pride in sporting events, and most important, they served as the focus for individual and collective aspirations.

In other respects, black schools were the instrument through which black professional educators discharged their responsibility to their community. Black educators labored to help students realize their achievement goals. In this role both principals and teachers were mere, but profound, extensions of the interests of the black community. Their professional and personal identity was organically tied to sources in the community network system, not to structures and agencies outside the community.

Desegregation struck at the heart of this social-institutional system in two ways. First, as Charles Johnson (1954) alluded, desegregation altered the unique institutional arrangements in the black community, particularly in the black schools. Second, the segregated schools in the black community were made to carry the burden of accommodating integration. Put more directly, black schools were the ones dismantled. Given the power imbalance between the contending groups, dismantling was a foregone conclusion because the Supreme Court remanded to the states and local school authorities the major responsibility for implementing its decree; the ultimate power to decide which schools were to be closed was in the hands of what Crain (1976) called "political men" not "rational" men (p. 338).

The desegregation process no longer ensured that those who taught or administered black children would represent black children's best interests. The number of black role models declined, and in their stead was placed a teaching and administrative staff that was either foreign to or overtly hostile to blacks. As James Haney (1978) commented:

> With more and more black educators leaving the classroom because of demotion, reassignment, or firing, black students will more than likely receive most if not all of their instructions from teachers who are not as familiar with their culture patterns as they should be; or as sympathetic in helping them obtain their educational objectives; or worse, who are actually prejudiced against their race (p. 94).

Desegregation has altered the concept of the collective whole, the collective struggle, and the collective will. There has been a transformation from valuing collective achievement to valuing individual achievement; that is, the individual is perceived as an independent entity who achieves success through merit and effort. Several factors have contributed to this transformation, the most obvious of which has to do with the fact that the educational environment of most black children does not reflect their primary cultural value system. This is to say, desegregated schools, with desegregated teacher staffs and administrations, are not likely to permit the expression of Afrocentric cultural traits and beliefs. The "well-adjusted," "good" black student is one who reflects in behavior and attitude a Eurocentric worldview, eschewing black behaviors and cultural preferences. The black child is urged to adopt a Eurocentric orientation toward achievement, viewing oneself as a singular unit responsible only to the self, placing the self at the center of one's world, and severing the affective ties to family and group in order to succeed.

Anderson (1988) explained:

> For children of color, biculturality is not a free choice, but a prerequisite for successful participation and eventual success. Non-white children generally are expected to be bicultural, bidialectic, or bicognitive; to measure their performance against a Euro-American yardstick; and to maintain this orientation. At the same time, they are being castigated whenever they attempt to express and validate their indigenous cultural and cognitive styles. Under such conditions cognitive conflict becomes the norm rather than the exception (p. 5).

To be sure, the situation for black children and the black community in general is most curious and paradoxical. The expected achievement gains for black children have not been fully realized, now thirty-five years into the desegregation process. The paradox is that the nurturing environment necessary for such achievement has been undermined by the very process designed to facilitate the desired educational benefits.

Disappearing Black Educators

Teachers. Education is now facing a second, somewhat different, crisis, related to black teachers. The issue today is not the callous, insensitive firing of black teachers, which followed the Brown decision, but the current inability of the profession to recruit and retain black teachers. Nowhere are the figures more startling than in the colleges of education at the historically black colleges, where the majority of black college graduates matriculate. In 1963, Florida A & M University graduated more than 300 education majors; in 1985 the number was less than 100 (Rodman, 1985). Garibaldi (1986) found that in 1976–1977, two black colleges in Louisiana awarded 33 percent and 41 percent of their total baccalaureate degrees to majors in education; in 1982–1983, these two institutions awarded 11 percent and 14 percent, respectively, of their degrees to majors in education. This trend is being reported by similar black institutions. A recent survey of ten southern states revealed that between 1980–1981 and 1983–1984, the number of black teachers declined by 5,000 or 6.4 percent. At the same time that the number of black teachers was decreasing, these ten southern states increased their total number of teachers by 3,300 (Rodman, 1985).

Many factors have contributed to the recent decline: (a) the general decline in the numbers of students who major in teacher education; (b) the decline in the number of black college students; (c) widening career options for blacks, especially black females; and (d) the institutionalization of teacher competency testing.

First, in the black and the white college populations, the number of students who declare education as a major has been decreasing since the early 1970s. In 1972–1973, the National Center for Education Statistics (NCES) reported 313,000 teacher education graduates. Ten years later the number declined to 45 percent (cited in Garibaldi, 1986). In 1966, 23 percent of blacks had an education major, which was by far the most popular major. By 1978 the number had dropped to 8.9 percent (Baratz, 1986). According to recent projections, massive teacher shortages are likely, and as many as one million teachers may be needed in the years 1989–1993 (Hawley, 1986). Hawley emphasized that these figures are not overestimated: the NCES predicted that 164,000 teachers would be needed in 1983; in fact, 230,000 were hired.

Second, the college attendance rate among black students is plummeting. Although blacks compose 13 percent of the eighteen to twenty-four-year-old population, they represent only 9.6 percent of students enrolled in college. In 1977 one-half of all black students were enrolled in college. This number fell to 36 percent by 1982 ("Blacks sliding backwards," 1985). When black students do attend college, 42 percent of them attend two-year institutions, and approximately 75 percent of blacks attending two-year colleges leave and never return. Fewer than 12 percent complete a four-year degree; fewer than 5 percent attend graduate or professional schools (Baratz, 1986; Zwerling, 1976).

The third factor is that black college students, particularly black females, have migrated from the teaching profession to fields perceived to be more financially and psychologically rewarding, more prestigious, and more accessible to rapid career advancement. Traditionally, teaching attracted large numbers of black and white women because it was considered appropriate "female work," tending and nurturing children. In addition, the hours and summer vacations were very compatible with teachers' own child-rearing responsibilities. These factors appear to be no longer so important. This generation is less likely to sex-type occupations, more likely to delay marriage and children, and more likely to be spouses in dual-career marriages in which men play a significant parenting role. For blacks, teaching is no longer one of the few occupations that lead to middle-class status. Black students' role models are more likely to be business executives in Fortune 500 companies, not schoolteachers or principals. The low pay of teachers is a further disincentive, and unwieldy school bureaucracies, with many mandated rules and regulations to govern teachers' and students' behavior, are also hindrances.

The number of black teachers will increase only when the achievement of at-risk black students increases. Teaching is a profession that has historically attracted the children of minorities, immigrants, and the working poor, who saw it as an entree to the middle class. A large percentage of black teacher education graduates of the sixties fit the broader "at risk" definition of the eighties. These black men and women, who are now in their forties and fifties, came from segregated schools of the South and North, were the first generation to attend college, were mostly low-income in economic terms but middle-class in values, and although bright, scored low on SAT and NTE (National Teachers Examination). If the profession is serious about increasing the numbers of black teachers, it must spend considerable effort to educate low-income black students at the preschool, elementary, and secondary levels. This group is the black pool that will yield the best return, not the middle-class children of black professionals. The children of the black middle class are preparing for medical, legal, and business careers, and the black community is not likely to encourage them to enter teacher education.

The fourth factor, the institutionalization of teacher competency tests, seems to be a greater threat to the survival of black teachers than do other factors. The results from teacher tests in several states and institutions may help in understanding the severity of the problem (Anrig, 1986).

In California, the passing rate for white test takers was 76 percent, but 26 percent for blacks; in Georgia, 87 percent of whites passed the test on the first try, while only 34 percent of the blacks did; in Oklahoma, there was a 79 percent pass rate for whites and 48 percent for blacks; in Florida, an 83 percent pass rate for whites, 35 percent for blacks; in Louisiana, 78 percent for whites, 15 percent for blacks; on the NTE Core Battery, 94 percent of whites passed, compared with 48 percent of blacks. Even more disheartening is the finding that teachers who fail on their initial try rarely pass on retakes (Rodman, 1986).

Concerned educators and their organizations have responded to this crisis with criticism concerning the tests' cultural bias, lack of content and predictive validity, and the inability of the tests to measure crucial affective qualities such as dedication, motivation, and caring. Additional responses include developing programs of remediation and test-taking skills for black students and challenging the use of these tests with legal suits and litigation. Nevertheless, some form of mandated teacher competency testing exists in forty-five of the fifty states, and the public sentiment to continue in this direction is strong. A 1986 Gallup Poll on education revealed that 85 percent of the public supported teacher competency tests. And now the profession is calling for national board exams.

The combined effect of these four factors is overwhelming, and future predictions are not encouraging. By 1990 the nation's minority teaching force could drop to 5 percent (from 12.5 percent in 1980) (J.P. Smith, 1988). "A minority teaching force of that size would mean that the average student, who has about 40 teachers during his precollegiate years, can expect at best to encounter only two teachers who are members of a minority group during his entire school career" (Smith, cited in Rodman, 1985, p. 1). The declines and predictions are most bleak in the southern states—where teachers were disproportionately dismissed after desegregation, where the teacher competency testing movement began and is most prevalent, where the majority of black children live, and where the prospects for future teacher employment and population growth are most promising.

The meaning of the reduction in the black teaching work force must be put in the context of other projections—by the turn of the century one-third of all public-school children will have minority group status (Cooper, 1988). Not only will these students be black or Hispanic, but they will also be at high risk for dropping out of school. Many will be economically disadvantaged or the children of single parents who are either unemployed or underemployed. The schools these children will attend will be schools in which teachers—both black and white—have traditionally not sought employment. It seems important that these at-risk students be taught by competent teachers who want to teach them, by a significant number of teachers who share their racial and cultural identity, and by teachers who are caring, patient, sensitive, and sympathetic.

Principals. The problems and solutions associated with educating black children and with increasing the number of black teachers are closely related to the essential administrative position, the principalship (see Chapter 5 for a discussion of the role of the school principal). Since the job requirements for school principals include prior teaching experience, it is clear that as the number of black teachers declines, so will the availability pool for principals and other administrators. The number of black principals has always been small because black principals were limited to serving in all-black schools prior to desegregation. After the 1954 Brown decision, black principals, like black teachers, were summarily dismissed, demoted, or otherwise reassigned. Data from the Association for the Study of Negro Life and History (Picott, 1976) revealed a 90 percent reduction in the number of black principals in the South after desegregation. Most of the black principals were relegated to jobs as assistant principals, whose primary duty was to discipline black children in the newly constituted, racially mixed schools (not an uncommon practice today). Others were reassigned as classroom teachers or special project directors in a central office with limited or no decision-making power.

Coursen (1975) reported a drastic reduction in the number of black principals in the following states: Alabama (in 1964, there were 134 black secondary principals, and in 1970 there only 14); Kentucky (by 1970 there were only 36 black principals , compared to 350 in 1954); Texas (the number of black principals decreased by 600 from 1964 through 1970); Virginia (in 1964, 107 black principals headed secondary schools, and in 1970 there were 16); and Delaware (black principals employed in Delaware fell from 50 in 1964 to 16 in 1970).

The most recent data on black representation in the principalship were published by the American Association of School Administrators (AASA) (Jones & Montenegro, 1988). The 1987–1988 survey reported that only 10 percent of all school principals were black, although black students will represent more than 16 percent of the total school population by the year 2020 (Pallas, Natriello, McDill, 1989).

The disappearance of the black principal from the schools that black children attended left the black community without one of its strongest role models, advocates, and spokespersons. Historically, the role of black principals was broader, more inclusive, and more varied in comparison with that of their white colleagues. This difference was due to the fact that black principals' personal and professional identities were inextricably related to the black community's aspirations for its youth, which set both the floor and the ceiling for black achievement and educational attainment.

Many descriptions of the relationship between black principals and the black community they served have been written (Jones, 1981; Sizemore, 1985; Sowell, 1976). The common denominators of black principals in varied communities "have been dedication to education, commitment to the children, and faith in what was possible to achieve" (Sowell, 1976, p. 53).

Billingsley (1968) conceived of leaders, such as principals, in the black community as follows:

In every aspect of the child's life a trusted elder, neighbor, Sunday school teacher, school teacher, or community member might instruct, discipline, assist, or otherwise guide the young of a given family. Second, as role models, community members show an example to and interest in the young people. Third, as advocates they actively intercede with major segments of society (a responsibility assumed by professional educators) to help young members of particular families find opportunities which might otherwise be closed to them. Fourth, as supportive figures, they simply inquire about the progress of the young, take a special interest in them. Fifth, in the formal roles of teacher, leader, elder, they serve youth generally as part of the general role or occupation (p. 99).

Billingsley's comments illustrate the expanded and crucial role of black educators, particularly black principals (Irvine & Irvine, 1983). Consequently, the displacement of black principals, whether resulting from political decisions related to desegregation or resulting from demographic variables related to a declining availability pool, affects not only the education profession but the total black community. This effect is so because the role of black principals within the institutional school structure has been formally eliminated and, perhaps more importantly, because the principal's function as an informal role model has been diminished or otherwise not made available to black students.

In summary, the distinct African-American culture of blacks can result in lack of correspondence between black students and their teachers, particularly as it relates to black students' presentation of self, their language, and their ways of knowing and processing information. The decreasing numbers of black teachers and principals will contribute to an increasing lack of synchronization between teachers and black students.

Lack of cultural sync leads to hidden conflict, hostility, infrequent communication, ineffective instruction, detachment, and negative teacher and student expectations. Teacher expectations are discussed in the next chapter.

3

Teacher Expectations

MODELS OF TEACHER EXPECTATIONS

No piece of educational research has generated as much attention among both the lay and the professional education community as Rosenthal and Jacobson's *Pygmalion in the Classroom* (1968). The media publicized the work widely but often misrepresented and oversimplified the findings. Rosenthal and Jacobson's research popularized the concept of teacher expectations as self-fulfilling prophecies and generated fifteen years of replications, critiques, and subsequent refinements and development of the theory.

Rosenthal and Jacobson's work took place in a lower-class elementary school. At the beginning of the school year, they administered Flanagan's Test of General Ability (TOGA) to eighteen students in the first through sixth grades. Teachers were told that the test was a newly developed instrument that would identify students who were "academic late bloomers."

Figure 3.1
Teacher and Student Expectations

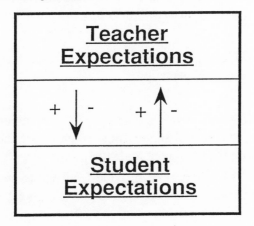

Approximately 20 percent of these students were randomly selected for an experimental group, and their names were given to their teachers as students whose test scores indicated that they would make large academic gains during the school year. The posttest of TOGA revealed that the experimental group gained four points, but even more dramatic was the fifteen-point gain of the first- and second-graders. The late bloomers also made significant gains in reading, and teachers perceived them to be more likely to succeed, more interesting, and more intellectually curious than the control group. Rosenthal and Jacobson concluded that the treatment contributed to raised teacher expectations and the subsequent enhanced performance of the children in the experimental group.

There are several models of the teacher expectation process. One of the most often referenced is the Brophy and Good Model (1974), which states the following:

> Early in the year, teachers form differential expectations for student performance. Consistent with these differential expectations, teachers behave differently toward different students. This differential teacher behavior communicates to each student something about how the student is expected to behave in the classroom and perform on academic tasks. If teacher treatment is consistent over time and if students do not actively resist or change it, the treatment will likely affect student self-concept, achievement motivation, level of aspiration, classroom conduct, and interactions with the teacher. These effects generally complement and reinforce the teacher's expectations, so that students conform to these expectations more than they might have otherwise. Ultimately, the expectations make a difference in student achievement and other outcomes, indicating that teacher expectations can function as self-fulfilling prophecies.

Rosenthal (1974; cited in Cooper, 1985) developed the following four-factor theory of teacher expectation:

1. Climate: Teachers should create warm socioemotional relationships with students. Teachers more often create these types of climates with their brighter students.

2. Feedback: Teachers should provide feedback to students about their performance. Teachers tend to praise high-expectation students and criticize low-expectation students.

3. Input: Teachers should teach quantitatively more material and qualitatively more challenging material. Students perceived as low-expectation receive fewer opportunities to learn and are taught less difficult material.

4. Output: Teachers should give students more opportunities to respond and ask questions. Teachers give preferential treatment by giving high-expectation students more clues, longer response times, and with more repeats, redirects, and rephrases.

Cooper's (1985) Expectation Communication Model is based on the idea that background and ability lead teachers to behave differently toward students and to have different expectations about academic performance. Classroom context, according to Cooper, is influenced by teachers' perceptions of the amount of control they have over the interaction initiator (teacher or student) and the setting (public or private). High-expectation students are successful regardless of the amount of control or the initiator of the interaction. On the other hand, this model states that low-expectation students succeed when teacher control is high, student initiations are few, and interactions take place privately rather than publicly. Finally, Cooper's model acknowledges the role that students' self-efficacy beliefs play in teacher expectations.

These models and subsequent research remind us that the original Rosenthal and Jacobson work was methodologically and conceptually oversimplistic. Methodologically, concerns have centered on the failure of other researchers to replicate Rosenthal and Jacobson's work in laboratory studies, classroom studies, or questionnaires. Other criticisms of teacher expectation research focus on the validity of nonclassroom research, the use of appropriate statistical analyses, instrumentation, observer reliability, the appropriate unit of observation (individual student or class), manipulation validity, the lack of manipulation of both positive and negative teacher expectations, the increasing transparency of teacher-expectation studies, prediction integration (the assimilation of new positive information with existing negative information), lack of generalizability, population representativeness, and ecological representativeness.

CONTEXTUAL AND SITUATIONAL VARIABLES

Conceptually, researchers in the early expectation studies ignored many contextual and situational variables that we now know are important mediators and factors that influence how expectations are communicated.

These variables include the grade level and the age of the student, the subject matter, the time of year, the characteristics of the teacher, and the characteristics of the student.

The Grade Level of the Student

Developmental theory suggests that students in middle and high schools are less influenced by teachers and more influenced by peers than are students in elementary schools. In addition, secondary students, compared with elementary students, have contact with different and more teachers during the school day, each perhaps with varying, possibly conflicting expectations. Elementary teachers have more contact and interactions with their students. Expectations vary significantly in relationship to the students' grade level.

The Subject Matter

In elementary schools, reading is more often taught in small, homogeneous ability groups, social studies and science in heterogeneous whole classes. It can be expected that teacher expectations for individual students vary if the reference for comparison is a small group of students with similar abilities or a large group of students with dissimilar abilities. The result is that certain subjects can be associated with different teacher expectations.

The Time of Year

According to Brophy (1985), teacher expectations are less rigid and inflexible at the beginning of the school year, but as the year progresses and teachers feel more pressure to complete the instructional objectives for the year, the self-fulfilling prophecy becomes operational.

The personal and cultural characteristics that the teacher and the student bring to the classroom context are important factors in the model, and they either contribute to or militate against black students' achievement. These two mediators are treated more extensively in the preceding chapter.

Teacher Characteristics

The role that teachers play in the school performance of black children is central and critical. Teachers' personal and cultural attributes as well as their attitudes and behaviors are important. However, the organizational and environmental context in which teachers perform their role and duties is an important feature that explicates teachers' essential influence and potency. Teachers exercise great flexibility in the content, the method of instruction, and the time spent on tasks. Unlike other organizations, schools do not adhere strictly to a bureaucratic model or the interdependent social systems theory. Performance is seldom monitored, standards are set but rarely enforced, the span of control is large and unwieldy, goals are diffuse and ambiguous, and coordination, predictability, and interdependence are low.

Weick (1982) popularized the phrase "loosely coupled systems" to describe the loose connections, isolation, flexibility, and the freedom that teachers have to make classroom decisions. Teachers often boast that the classroom door is designed to keep children in as well as to keep others out. Once that door closes, teachers make the final decisions about the content, the method, and the materials they teach.

An example of this phenomenon was cited in a study by Berliner (1984) in which one elementary teacher was observed for ninety days. During that time, the teacher taught nothing about fractions, in spite of the fact that coverage of the topic was state-mandated. When asked why she did not teach fractions, the teacher replied, "I don't like fractions!" Another example Berliner cited is the study in which an elementary teacher who reported she liked science taught twenty-eight times more science than the teacher who said she disliked the subject. The stated curriculum seems to be taught in a broad and rather discretionary way by teachers who are left alone to make decisions as to who and what will be taught.

Teachers socialize and condition students through the hidden and the stated curriculum. They consciously and unconsciously inculcate students for their appropriate role in the institution by delivering messages, sanctions, and rewards about appropriate behaviors and expectations. This inculcation is so powerful and effective because the relationship between a teacher and a student rivals the relationship between a parent and a child. Jackson (1983) estimated that from the time a child enters kindergarten until the child enters junior high school, he/she spends more than seven thousand hours in school. Jackson continued, "From the age of six onward, he is a more familiar sight to his teacher than his father, and possibly even to his mother" (p. 30). One of Jackson's observations is particularly intriguing: a child would have to attend a one-hour church service every Sunday for 150 years before the inside of a church became as familiar as the inside of a school.

Teacher influence does not end in junior high. When high school students were asked who or what had influenced them to become the kind of people they were, 58 percent named one teacher or more (Csikszentmihalyi & McCormack, 1986).

Not only do teachers influence students' achievement and their cognitive development, but they influence self-concept and attitudes as well. Students identify teachers as significant others in their lives, and how a child feels about himself or herself is to a large extent determined by the child's perceptions of how the teacher feels about him/her. Students' perceptions of their teachers' feelings toward them have been found to be highly correlated with the students' self-concept. Many children who believe they are not liked by their teachers do not like themselves or school. These students feel isolated, discouraged, and eventually fail academically. This effect is exaggerated for low-income and minority students because they are more teacher-dependent and are more likely to hold the teacher in high esteem than middle-class students do (Coleman, 1966). Unfortunately, teachers may not reciprocate, preferring children who are more Anglo and middle-class (Peck, Manning, & Buntain, 1977).

It is pertinent to note that teacher warmth, affect, and enthusiasm are important attributes and have been found to be highly correlated with student achievement. When 813 minority, low-income adults, aged eighteen to thirty-four, were asked to identify the characteristics of the teachers who had influenced them the most, they most often selected teachers' social and interpersonal skills, affective characteristics, and temperament. The former students chose the following descriptors to portray these influential teachers: approachable, pleasant, easy to relate to, accepting, tolerant, helpful, concerned, caring, thoughtful, and perceptive of and sensitive to the needs of students. Johnson and Prom-Johnson (1986) concluded, "It appears that while talented students are strongly influenced toward growth and development during the school years, the way in which this happens is through the interpersonal skills and affective characteristics of good teachers" (p. 279). Similarly, in an ethnographic study by St. John (1971), black children improved their conduct and school attendance when taught by a child-oriented rather than a task-oriented teacher—a teacher who was kind, optimistic, understanding, adaptable, and warm. In another study, a researcher (Kleinfeld, 1972) found that for white students, parents' perceived evaluation was more strongly related to the students' academic self-concept than was teachers' perceived evaluation. However, for black students, it was the teachers' perceived evaluation that was more strongly related to the students' academic self-concept.

Part of the puzzle of black nonachievement has to be related to this predicament: some teachers are in classrooms with black and low-income students whom they prefer not to teach and, even worse, do not like as individuals. Holliday (1985) asked twenty-four teachers to rate forty-four black students on reading, math, oral language, spelling, written language, handwriting, and classroom behavior. The students also rated themselves on these traits. Black children's achievement was minimally influenced by their own perceptions but significantly influenced by the teacher's perceptions. This finding is particularly relevant because researchers have found that black and other minority pupils are more negatively affected by teacher expectations than white students are (Baker, 1973; Krupczak, 1972; Yee, 1968). Bruno and Doscher (1981) found that the higher the percentage of black students in a school, the "less attractive" the school was described by teachers and the higher the number of requests for teacher transfers.

In summary, teachers are significant others in their students' lives; as significant others, they affect the achievement and self-concept of their students, particularly black students. Because schools are loosely coupled systems and teachers frequently operate autonomously and independently, teachers' impact on the lives of students is perhaps greater than one might imagine.

It would indeed be unfair to imply that teachers are solely a product of their own cultural/racial reference group. Cultural identity as well as individual characteristics determine attitudes and behaviors. Although they do not share cultural and racial identities with black students, some white teachers are effective with black students because of their personal traits and teaching expertise.

Some teacher traits and characteristics that researchers have noted as influential in mediating teacher expectations include the following (Brophy, 1985; Jussim, 1986):

- ability to deal constructively with failure
- willingness to take personal responsibility for student progress
- beliefs about achievement and the nature of intelligence tests
- perception about personal control over students
- rigidity or flexibility of their expectations
- general intelligence
- cognitive complexity
- locus of control
- sense of efficacy
- cognitive style
- tolerance for ambiguity

- degree of prejudice and discriminatory behavior
- coping and defense mechanisms
- degree of dogmatism
- beliefs about the role of teachers

Brophy and Good (1974) concluded that teachers' susceptibility to teacher expectation effects is a function of individual teacher differences. Specifically, they characterized teachers as proactive, reactive, or over-reactive. Overreactive teachers treat students as stereotypes rather than as individuals. This kind of teacher is more likely to show favoritism to high-achieving, middle-class students and reject culturally different students. The reactive teacher is more flexible and accurate in expectations but allows the students to control teacher-student interactions in the classroom. In other words, these teachers react to differences in students' performance and behavior and maintain the existing differences between high and low achievers or black and white students. Proactive teachers do not operate out of stereotypes or differences in students' performance and behavior but rely on their training, experience, and beliefs to structure appropriate learning goals for high and low achievers. These teachers' expectations are usually accurate and flexible.

Student Characteristics

By the time students enroll in kindergarten, they have well-developed personality traits and characteristics, attitudes, perceptions, and predispositions toward learning, all of which individual teachers either prefer or dislike. Although seldom recognized or publicly admitted, teachers do favor some students and treat them preferentially in their classrooms, and students are aware of teachers' partial behaviors (Weinstein 1985).

What kind of student do teachers prefer to teach and interact with? Kedar-Voivodas's review (1983) of the works of Brophy and Evertson (1981), Brophy and Good (1974), Good and Brophy (1978), Silberman (1969), and Willis and Brophy (1974) provides some insight into the student characteristics that influence teacher-student interactions. All these researchers asked teachers to nominate one child from their classes to each of the following categories: (a) attachment: students whom teachers would choose to keep another year for the sheer joy of it; (b) rejection: students whom teachers would be relieved to have removed from their classes, if the class size would be reduced; (c) indifference: students whom teachers feel least prepared to talk about if the students' parents dropped in unannounced for a conference; and (d) concern: students whom teachers feel a good deal of concern for and to whom they would like to devote all their attention, if they could.

Attachment students were bright, academically talented students who were obedient and cooperative and did not cause trouble in the classroom. They seemed to be always prepared and well disciplined and made no excessive demands on the teachers' time or energy. Their contacts, both self- and teacher-initiated, were academic rather than procedural. Rejected students were the exact opposite of attachment students. They ignored the rules and were defiant, belligerent, and aggressive with teachers and their peers. Their interactions with teachers were disciplinary in nature, that is, interactions in which the teachers criticized these students' behaviors. Although perceived to be low achievers, the rejected students were actually no different from other students in academic achievement. Teachers interpreted their demand for attention as inappropriate, and their legitimate requests were frequently denied. Concerned students had learning problems, but because they behaved appropriately, teachers were eager to assist them. Unlike the rejected students, concerned students were academically inferior to their peers. Indifferent students were seldom noticed, often ignored and forgotten, passive, and described by teachers as unattractive and introverted. Although very little research has been done on how race affects the students' nomination into these categories, Brophy and Evertson (1981) reported that girls in the indifferent and the concerned groups were more likely to be nonwhite and that boys in the rejection group were more likely to be nonwhite.

Feshbach (1969) discovered that teachers most preferred to teach rigid, conforming, orderly students and least preferred active, independent, and assertive children. A social class dimension seems evident in these preferences. In 1984, 47 percent of a sample of teachers in Dade County, Florida, said they preferred "nice kids from average homes who are respectful and hard-working"; only 14 percent preferred "underprivileged students from difficult or deprived homes for whom school can be a major opportunity" (Kottkamp, Provenzo, & Cohn, 1986, p. 562).

When this author asked a class of preservice and in-service teachers in Atlanta, Georgia, to describe their favorite student, most of the teachers described a student who was above average in achievement, well mannered, and cooperative. The "favorite" student's profile included characteristics such as friendly, sense of humor, smiles a lot, enthusiastic, active participant in class discussions, caring, curious, animated, affectionate, outgoing, inquisitive, bouncy, energetic, and playful. Clearly this extroverted achiever was preferred to other types of personalities.

Interestingly, this Atlanta survey emphasizes an important point, one that is often overlooked in teacher-student relationships. That is, teachers like students who like them. Those students who let teachers know that they are liked, valued, needed, and appreciated engender the affections of the teachers, who subsequently spend more instructional time with them.

Some of the following comments from teachers in the Atlanta survey illustrate this phenomenon:

- "My favorite student [a five-year-old] tries his best to please me and is always trying to find ways to get my attention. He is very bright and will probably be successful because he has already figured out that he has to do what the teacher wants in order to please her."

- "I found that I prefer to teach a more physically attractive kid. Usually one that follows directions well. Most important, I like the ones that respond to me."

- "The child I like to work with best is a little girl who is extremely bright and outgoing. Part of the reason I started to like her the best was because for the first few weeks she was the only one who knew my name."

- "I like working with Matt the best. He is well-behaved and doesn't act up. He does what he is told and gives me no problems. He is very soft-spoken and tries so hard to please me."

- "She is a beautiful child—short, cute, big brown eyes that always sparkle when she talks. She is lovable and will always come up and give me a hug or tell me a story."

- "My favorite student is a junior general chemistry student. She is lively, vivacious, friendly, and warm. I think the reason I prefer her to most of my other students is that she is very empathetic. She treats me like a real person instead of a servant."

- "I like to work with a very quiet boy because he does his work and knows his material. He respects my authority and tries to pamper me."

Meta-analysis by Dusek and Joseph (1985) supports these teacher descriptions of preferred students. They found that teachers prefer physically attractive, white, middle-class students and have higher expectations for students who are well behaved, controlled, obedient, and attentive. Teachers are influenced by information in students' cumulative folder such as comments of previous teachers, family background information, and photographs. There is some evidence that teachers make more favorable judgments about students who have common or frequently used names than about students who have unusual names, and their expectations are influenced (positively or negatively) by prior contact with the siblings of their students. Finally, teachers prefer students who exhibit traditional sex role behaviors.

Some students bring to the instructional setting personal beliefs about their efficacy which make them more resistant and less susceptible to the effects of teacher expectancy. Students who have healthy self-images, high self-expectations, and an internal as opposed to an external locus of control, students who dismiss teachers as insignificant others in their lives, and students who are intellectually able, active, salient, and persistent are able to mediate negative teacher expectations and attitudes. Black children, however, have difficulty mediating teachers' negative expectations because they cannot alter their race, class, family background, perceptions of their skin color as unattractive, the behavior of their siblings, and their often unusual names. Racism, discrimination, and the general devaluation of black people and their culture have also limited black children's development of a healthy sense of self, high expectations, and inner-directed orientations.

Brophy (1985) has attempted to deemphasize the role that teacher expectations play in teacher-student interactions and subsequent student achievement. He stated that most teachers' perceptions of students are accurate and reality-based—not based on stereotypes and false information. Further, Brophy believes that most teachers who receive false data on students correct these inaccuracies as soon as more dependable information becomes available. Finally, Brophy believes that teacher expectations only minimally affect student achievement.

Hall and Merkel (1985) stated:

We have come full circle from suggesting that differential expectations of students with different abilities were causing differential treatment, which in turn resulted in insufficient progress and perpetuating a caste system based on social class, to the conclusion that these differential treatments are actually beneficial to all concerned. It should be mentioned that this latter conclusion is not one suggested by only a single author. Brophy (1979) on a number of occasions and Good (1981) have suggested similar kinds of differences in teacher behavior when dealing with students of differing ability and/or social class (p. 85).

Good (1981) concluded that the most accurate statement about teacher expectations is that they sustain differences in student performance levels, even though they rarely create these differences. Brattesani, Weinstein, and Marshall (1984) disagreed. They concluded that teacher expectations do not merely sustain preexisting differences in student achievement but also increase these differences. These researchers stated, "Our findings are consistent with the hypothesis that teachers can behave in ways that communicate their achievement expectations to their students (expectations that may deviate from a student's prior achievement), that students perceive these expectations from teachers' behavior, and that these expectations influence students' own expectations and achievement" (p. 248).

The disagreements about teacher expectations research center around methodology, procedure, and analysis rather than around the question of whether a relationship exists between teacher expectations and student outcomes (Rist, 1987). Braun (1976) concluded in his review of the literature that there is "convincing, if not unequivocal support of the expectancy hypothesis" (p. 189).

TEACHER EXPECTATIONS—IS RACE OPERATIVE?

Teachers often remark that they are not consciously aware of the race of the students they teach. Some believe that it is preferable to see students' skin color as neutral rather than to acknowledge their black or white racial identities. Other teachers believe, as reported by Bennett (1986), that the recognition of a person's race is racist. By ignoring students' most obvious physical characteristic, race, these teachers are also disregarding students' unique cultural behaviors, beliefs, and perceptions—important factors that teachers should incorporate, not eliminate, in their instructional strategies and individualized approaches to learning. When teachers ignore students' race and claim that they treat all children the same, they usually mean that their model of the ideal student is white and middle-class and that all students are treated as if they are or should be both white and middle-class. Such treatment contributes to perceptions of inferiority about black culture and life and to denial and self-hatred by black children. Second, teachers, like all humans, notice the elements of initial human interactions that are the most obvious—sex, race, and physical appearance (Synder, 1982). Perceived similarities in physical appearance and values lead to initial personal attraction and subsequent friendships. It is not coincidental that friends most often share race, intelligence, social class, and education. White middle-class teachers and low-income black males are likely initially to hold negative impressions of each other. Teachers must move beyond their initial impressions and refrain from selectively reinforcing their stereotypic thinking by cataloging information that confirms their first impressions and by dismissing or ignoring contradictory data that produce cognitive dissonance.

Lightfoot (1978) confirmed this point:

Even if one moves beyond the broad societal tendencies to exclude children from economic participation and serious personhood, there are general tendencies of teachers not to see individual children but to see them as members of prescribed sociological categories. Teachers, like all of us, use the dimensions of class, race, sex, ethnicity to bring order to their perception of the classroom environment. Rather than teachers gaining a more in-depth and holistic understanding of the child, with the passage of time teachers' perceptions become increasingly stereotyped and children become hardened caricatures of an initial discriminatory vision (pp. 85–86).

Brophy and Evertson's (1981) comments on teachers' reactions to students' race are indeed curious. Their viewpoint is that teachers do not systematically respond to students' race but that teachers respond to students' behavior.

Teachers respond to students' personal characteristics and classroom behavior, not group membership. Where group differences are observed, it is because certain behavioral differences in students are systematically associated with group membership. However, individuals who are exceptions to group norms are treated differently. More generally, teachers usually deal with students individually and not as members of groups (p. 48).

What Brophy and Evertson seem to imply is that when black students behave in ways different from or contrary to black cultural norms, teachers treat them as individuals. But what happens when black children behave in ways consistent with their cultural socialization, as most children, black or white, do? The inference is that teachers may treat them as stereotypic members of their racial group. Why should black students bear the responsibility and burden of behaving in ways that are exceptions to their group norms in order to be treated as individuals? Majority group children have no such modifiers or qualifiers on their manner of self-presentation and behavior.

Baron, Tom, and Cooper (1985) concluded after a review of the research that teachers have more positive expectations for white students than for black students. The student's race or class cues teachers to apply generalized expectations, which make it difficult for teachers to develop specific expectations for individual black students. They posited that, indeed, the student's race is a dominant factor in teacher expectations and that this situation makes it very difficult for minority students, whose burden is to distinguish themselves from generalized expectations about their racial group.

This "guilt by association" implies that black students must demonstrate to teachers that the negative stereotypes generally associated with black students' behavior do not pertain to them. This imposed denial and refutation of one's cultural heritage and racial identity are directly related to black self-hatred, lowered self-esteem, and heightened anxiety and possibly to lower academic achievement.

A review of research by this author (Irvine, 1988b) on teacher expectations as related to teacher and student race has revealed that teachers, particularly white teachers, have more negative expectations for black students than for white students. The research methodologies of the studies reviewed are categorized as experimental studies, naturalistic setting studies, and teacher perception and attitude studies. Of the thirty-six studies reviewed, five were experimental studies in which variables were manipulated by experimenters (see Table 3.1). The teachers in these studies were told to expect a certain achievement performance from the students. The studies found that whites received more favorable communications than blacks, but the studies vary in design and methodology, and they are difficult to replicate, interpret, and generalize.

One of the most often cited of these studies was conducted by Rubovits and Maehr (1973). Using sixty-six "teachers" (white female undergraduates) in a simulated teaching group of four students—two blacks and two whites—these teachers were told that one of each race was "gifted." The results, which the researchers called "a disturbing instance of white racism," indicated that the white gifted received more praise than the black gifted and that gifted blacks received more criticism than any other group. Generally, white teachers gave blacks less attention, less encouragement, less praise, and more criticism. In addition, teachers ignored more of the statements made by black students. Perhaps these teachers experienced dissonance about these gifted black males because they did not confirm their expectations of black children as nonachievers.

Taylor (1979) investigated how students' race and sex interacted with pupil ability to affect teacher behavior. In the study, 100 white female undergraduates in a teacher training program presented lessons to "phantom" students, who were alleged to be observing and responding from behind a two-way glass. The students were described as high- or low-ability, male or female, and black or white. The verbal and nonverbal teacher responses were recorded. Taylor discovered that the subjects who believed their pupils were black gave fewer positive feedback statements after correct responses and fewer helpful slips of the tongue that gave away answers than did the subjects who thought their pupils were white. Taylor also found that the subjects in the black male and white female groups were less likely to offer their pupils either kind of assistance—positive feedback or helpful slips. Positive feedback and helpful slips were most often withheld from black males and most often given to white males.

Table 3.1
Experimental Studies (Non-classroom)

First author	Year	Expectation Measure	Race Student w/ Higher Exp.	Race of Biased Teacher
Coates	1972	verbal feedback	white	white (male)
Rubovits	1973	verbal	white	white
Word	1974	nonverbal interaction	no whites in study BL lower class	white
Feldman	1979	nonverbal interaction	same as teacher	same as student
Taylor	1979	positive	white	white

In eighteen studies, teachers' attitudes toward and perceptions of black students have been compared with those for white students (see Table 3.2). Again, researchers of these studies concluded that teachers had more negative attitudes and beliefs about black children than about white children in such variables as personality traits and characteristics, ability, language, behavior, and potential. In one study, Gottlieb (1964) asked black and white teachers from six inner-city schools to rate the students they taught. These teachers were given a list of thirty-six adjectives and

Table 3.2
Teacher Perceptions and Attitudes

First author	Year	Expectation Measure	Race Student w/ Higher Exp.	Race of Biased Teacher
Gottlieb	1964	Personality traits	White	White
Yees	1968	Personality traits	White	Not given
Datta	1968	Personality traits	White	Not given
Leacock	1969	Personality trait	White	Not given
Guskin	1970	Language	White	White
Howe	1971	Ability	White	White
Williams	1970	Language	White	White
Braxton	1972	Behavior	White	White
Woodward	1971	Language	White	Not given
Eaves	1975	Behavior	White	White
Harvey	1975	Ability	Whte	White
Lietz	1978	Behavior	White	Not given
Griffin	1979	Ability	White	White
Cornbleth	1980	Potential achievement	White	White
		Personality traits	White	White
Washington	1980	Personality characteristics	White	No difference
Scott	1980	Personality characteristics	White	White
Aloia	1981	Ability	White	Not given
Washington	1982	Ability	White	White
		Physical appearance	White	Black

asked to select the adjectives that best described their students. Black teachers described the students as happy, energetic, and fun-loving; their white counterparts described these same children as talkative, lazy, and rebellious. Griffin and London (1979) administered a questionnaire to 270 black and white teachers in inner-city schools in which 90 percent or more of the children enrolled were members of minority groups. The researchers found that 64.6 percent of the black teachers considered minority students of average or better ability; 66.1 percent of the white teachers considered these same children to be of average or lesser ability.

The most methodologically sound studies are the twelve that were conducted in naturalistic classroom settings (see Table 3.3). Brophy (1983) and Brophy and Good (1974) concluded that these studies are more valid because the results come from teacher expectations that were formed naturally, rather than coming from questionnaires or experiments in which expectations were induced from contrived information about students. In addition, these studies are more generalizable and have more external validity than experimental studies.

Simpson and Erickson (1983) observed teachers' verbal and nonverbal behaviors for the independent variables of student race, student gender, and teacher gender. The white teachers directed more verbal praise, criticism, and nonverbal praise toward males than toward females. In contrast, they directed more nonverbal criticism toward black males than toward black females, white females, or white males. Aaron and Powell (1982) also found that black pupils received more negative academic and behavioral feedback than did white pupils.

Corollary studies in which it was concluded that black students have fewer favorable interactions with teachers than white children do include the work of Peck (1977), Byers and Byers (1972), Katz (1973), Hillman and Davenport (1978), Barnes (1978), and Washington (1980). No differences in treatment were found by Meyer and Lindstrom (1969), Barnes (1978), Cornbleth and Korth (1980), and Aaron and Powell (1982). In studies conducted by Brown, Payne, Lankewich, and Cornell (1970) and Byalick and Bersoff (1974), teachers gave more praise and less criticism to students of the opposite race.

Some of these studies were conducted in naturalistic classroom settings and others in experimental settings, and some were ratings on teacher perception questionnaires. The following factors warrant cautious interpretation: race, gender, socioeconomic class, behavior, achievement, personality, and attractiveness. The grade levels (K–12) varied, as did the years of experience of the teacher, the sample size, the instruments and questionnaires used to collect data, and the voluntary or involuntary participation of subjects. More important, a number of studies did not take into account differing racial representation within each classroom. However, the data do seem to imply that in these three types of studies, white teachers had more negative expectations for black students than did black teachers.

Table 3.3
Naturalistic Classroom Studies

First author	Year	Expectation Measure	Race Student w/ Higher Exp.	Race of Biased Teacher
Meyer	1969	Verbal Approval	No difference (ND)	ND
Peck	1977	Grades	White	Black
Brown	1970	Praise/Criticism	Opposite race of teacher	Same as student
Byers	1972	Eye contact	White	White
		Nonverbal initiation		
Katz	1973	Verbal initiation	White	Not given
Byalick	1974	Positive verbal reinforcement	Opposite of teacher	Same as student
	1974	Touching	Same as teacher	Same as student
Barnes	1978	Verbal interaction	ND	ND
Barnes	1978	Higher level questions	White	White
Hillman	1978	Verbal interaction	White	ND
Cornbleth	1980	Verbal interaction	ND	ND
Washington	1980	Positive feedback	Black	White
		Negative feedback	White	White
Aaron	1982	Positive feedback	ND	ND
	1982	Negative feedback	White	White
	1982	Academic feedback	White	White
Simpson	1983	Nonverbal criticism	White	White

Do black teachers, who are middle-class by virtue of their profession, discriminate against lower-class black children? Some do, but black teachers share with black students their racial identities and critical cultural similarities. On the other hand, white teachers share neither culture nor racial identity.

In addition to their having more positive expectations, it appears that black teachers serve as advocates of black children. In a not yet published book, Meier, Steward, and England's (cited in Snider, 1987) analysis of 173 large urban school districts found that as the proportion of black teachers in a school district increases, the proportion of black students assigned to special education classes, suspended, or expelled decreases. Meier speculated that black teachers are less willing to conclude that black students are not teachable in regular classrooms.

In summary, teacher expectations are powerful contributors to the school achievement of black students but are mediated by factors such as the characteristics of the teacher and the students. It does appear that black children are particularly susceptible to negative teacher expectations because they differ from most teachers who are white and middle-class; they are also more teacher-dependent. Previous research, most importantly naturalistic classroom studies, documents that white teachers are more likely to have more negative expectations for black students than do black teachers.

Do the conclusions of this paper suggest that all white teachers are ineffective teachers of black children or that all black teachers are effective teachers of black children? Certainly not. What is suggested is that as a group white teachers are more likely than black teachers to hold negative expectations for black children and that white teachers are more likely than black teachers to be out of cultural sync with the black students they teach. These conclusions do not ignore the fact that some white teachers are excellent teachers of black children or that some black teachers are ineffective with black children, treating them with disdain and hostility.

4

Research on Teacher-
Student Interactions:
Effects of Student Race,
Gender, and Grade Level

The limitations of previous teacher expectation research were addressed in a study (Irvine, 1986) conducted by this author. The study examined (a) the quantity and quality of teachers' verbal feedback statements to students; (b) the initiating behaviors of students; and (c) the public response opportunities available to students. These issues were discussed in relation to the student's race, gender, and grade level or age.

TEACHER VERBAL FEEDBACK

The naturalistic classroom studies reviewed in the previous chapter (see Table 3.3) concluded that teachers' verbal feedback statements do vary according to the student's race. A majority of the studies showed that teachers deliver more negative feedback to black students than to white students. Some studies, however, showed no difference in teacher verbal feedback by race, and some studies found that teachers favored students of the opposite race.

Teachers also interact differentially toward students based on gender. Quantitatively, the research indicates that boys interact more with teachers than do girls (Brophy & Good, 1970; Martin, 1972). According to a review of the literature sponsored by the National Institute of Education (Safilios-Rothschild, 1979), the quality of these communications seems to be critical. Boys tend to be criticized more frequently than girls (Datta, Schaefer, & Davis, 1968; Dweck & Bush, 1976; Felsenthal, 1970; Jackson & Lahaderne, 1967; Lippitt & Gold, 1959), and teachers are more likely to use a harsh tone when criticizing boys (Jackson & Lahaderne, 1967;

Waetjen, 1962). Interestingly, in some studies teachers who were more critical of boys than girls also praised them more than they praised girls (Felsenthal, 1970; Meyer & Lindstrom, 1969; Meyer & Thompson, 1956).

Brophy and Evertson (1981) found that boys had more contact with teachers because their behaviors elicited more communications. In addition, teachers elicited more academic and personal contact with boys than with girls. Student gender accounted for a significant difference in the amount of teacher criticism; however, there was no significant difference between teacher praise directed toward males and that directed toward females.

The grade level of the student is also related to the interaction/communications process. Brophy and Evertson (1981) observed more small-group instruction and brief seat-work assignments in the lower elementary grades, specifically grades 2 and 3. Under these conditions, one might speculate that verbal feedback statements would be frequent and individualized. The fourth and fifth grades use fewer small-group instructional settings and more whole-class instruction. These older students are involved in more independent study and extended seat-work assignments; consequently, they are probably involved in fewer interactions with the teacher.

There are fewer behavioral contacts in the upper elementary grades than in the early elementary grades. Teachers concentrate on socializing younger children to the pupil role by communicating pleasure or displeasure for behaviors and responses exhibited by pupils. By the time a student has entered the fourth grade, fewer conditioning responses are needed.

STUDENT INITIATING BEHAVIORS

Teacher-student interaction is a two-way process; students and teachers influence each other's behaviors. Students condition teachers' behavior as much as teachers condition students' behavior. Brophy and Evertson (1981) stated that this process is not a one-sided relationship between an active, initiating teacher and a passive, responding student. This area of research, however, has not been extensively reviewed in the literature. How individual students and their personality characteristics mediate teacher expectations is not clearly understood. Brophy (1983) did report that the more active, initiating, and salient student is more likely to be perceived accurately by the teacher. Less salient students behave in ways that sustain inappropriate teacher expectations because their contact with the teacher is infrequent and because the teacher knows very little about the student. Although teacher-student interaction is a two-way process, it is by no means an equal process. Teachers exert control and influence over students more systematically and more effectively than students do over teachers.

Research has not revealed any differences in initiating behavior because of student race per se, but Katz (1973) found that white students initiated more interactions with teachers than did black students in integrated classrooms and that teachers apparently either passively accepted or actively reinforced the trend.

Students in the middle years are more likely to initiate interactions with their teachers than are students in the early elementary grades (Brophy & Evertson, 1981). These initiations are frequently "call outs," which teachers are more inclined to accept from older students than from younger students. Brophy and Evertson speculated that teachers are more oriented toward whole-class activities in the middle years and that the teacher gives higher priority to the group's academic progression than to providing equal opportunities for each student to participate. Consequently, call outs occur more frequently in the middle grades than in the early elementary years.

PUBLIC RESPONSE OPPORTUNITIES

Research evidence suggests that students do not have equal numbers of opportunities to respond publicly in the classroom. Good (1970) presented some of the subtle processes that predispose teachers to call on one group of students more often than on another group. "A teacher who solicits responses from pupils does not haphazardly pose questions and randomly focus on one of the many waving hands. The teacher has a reason for asking questions, and she tries to call on pupils who are capable of satisfying this purpose" (p. 193). He concluded that low achievers have fewer chances to respond publicly in the classroom than do high achievers. Teachers who want to encourage or motivate a class seem to avoid calling on a student who might give an inappropriate response. Teachers who elicit personal gratification call on students who are high achievers, and they ignore low achievers. According to Good, teachers sometimes fail to provide response opportunities to low achievers because they wish to avoid raising the anxiety level of low achievers or embarrassing them in front of their peers.

In another study (Good & Dembo, 1973), 96 percent of the teachers who responded to a questionnaire revealed that they preferred calling on low achievers only when they were confident that these students would give the correct response. In addition, 34 percent of the teachers in the study believed that low achievers should be called on less frequently than other students.

Other research findings suggest that boys are more likely to be provided public response opportunities than are girls (Brophy & Evertson, 1981; Brophy & Good, 1974). Because boys are active, salient, and perceived by teachers as potentially disruptive, they are frequently provided response opportunities as a method of maintaining appropriate classroom discipline. On the other hand, because of the compliance and inactivity of female students, they are called on less often and given fewer opportunities to respond. Little data exists as to how response opportunities vary by grade level. Generally, there are more public response opportunities in the middle years than in the early elementary years because of "the increasing emphasis on recitations and discussions, in which teachers call on students to respond to questions" (Brophy & Evertson, 1981, p. 103).

The relationship between student race and the frequency of response opportunities has rarely been investigated; the few studies investigating the topic have not yielded consistent findings. Rubovits and Maehr (1973) and Jackson and Cosca (1974) found that teachers called on minority students less often. However, Aaron and Powell (1982) and Barnes (1978) found no significant difference between the public contacts that teachers initiated with black and with white students.

Teachers' verbal feedback communications to students seem to be influenced by the race, gender, and grade of the student. According to most of the studies, black students receive less favorable interactions than do white children. Male students interact more with teachers than female students, academically and personally. Upper elementary students receive fewer feedback statements than lower elementary students do, but that difference is partly because upper elementary students require fewer behavioral contacts.

More active, salient students are more likely to initiate contacts with teachers. Boys are more active than girls; hence, they initiate more interactions. Students in the middle years are more initiating than students in the early elementary grades. Only one study (Katz, 1973) indicates that student initiating behaviors differ by student race. This study revealed that in integrated classrooms white students initiated more interactions than black students.

In summary, research findings suggest that boys are more likely to be provided public response opportunities than are girls, and more response opportunities are provided in upper elementary grades than in the lower

elementary grades. The findings concerning the student's race are contradictory.

RESEARCH QUESTIONS

This study examined teacher-student interactions as related to the
students' race, gender, and grade level. Specifically, the following questions were posed:

1. Do the quantity and the quality of teacher feedback statements to
   students differ significantly according to student race, student
   gender, and student grade level?
2. Do the positive and the negative student initiating behaviors
   differ significantly according to student race, student gender, and
   student grade level?
3. Does the frequency of response opportunities for students differ
   significantly according to student race, student gender, and student grade level?

METHODOLOGY

For a complete description of the research methodology, including unit
of analysis, the observers, training, instrumentation, operational definitions of communication interaction variables, experimental design, means
and standard deviations table for feedback categories, and table of analyses
of variance, see the Appendix.

The communication interaction data were collected in sixty-three classrooms in ten schools in four public school systems. The grades included
lower elementary (LE) grades K-2 and upper elementary (UE) grades 3–5.

INSTRUMENTATION

The instrument was a modification of the Brophy–Good Dyadic Interaction System. The instrument used the following interaction categories:

Teacher Verbal Feedback Statements

1. Positive—statements of praise and affirmations of correct
   responses

2. Neutral—routine repetition of student's answer, teacher's procedural statements, or related questions

3. Negative—statements of criticism and negation of incorrect responses

4. Total communication—quantitative combination of the positive, negative, and neutral categories.

Student Initiating Behaviors

1. Positive—voluntary student initiation

2. Negative—nonvoluntary student initiation

Public Response Opportunities

Number of opportunities that students have to respond in the classroom as the result of the teacher's calling on the student.

RESULTS

Table 4.1 summarizes the results of the analysis of variance.

Positive Teacher Feedback

Upper elementary (UE, grades 3–5) black females received less positive teacher feedback than did lower elementary (LE, grades K–2) white males and less than upper elementary black males. Lower elementary black females received less positive feedback than did LE white males and less than UE black males. Upper elementary and lower elementary white females received less positive feedback than did UE black males.

Neutral Teacher Feedback

There were no significant effects concerning neutral teacher feedback.

Negative Teacher Feedback

Male students received significantly more negative feedback than did female students.

Table 4.1
Summary of Findings

1. **Positive**
    - UE and LE black females < LE white males and UE
      black males
    - UE and LE white females < UE black males
2. **Neutral**
    - No Difference
3. **Negative**
    - Males > Females
4. **Total Communications**
    - LE and UE white females < LE black males, black
      females, and white males; UE black and white
      males
5. **Academic**
    - In UE, females < males
6. **Non-academic**
    - Males > Females
    - LE > UE

<u>**Initiating Behaviors**</u>

1. **Positive**
    - Males > Females
2. **Negative**
    - Males > Females

<u>**Response Opportunities**</u>

- UE black females < LE black females

Total Teacher Communications

The combined three categories (positive, neutral, and negative) resulted
in a significant interaction. LE white females received significantly less
feedback than LE black males, LE black females, UE white males, UE
black males, and LE white males. UE white females received less feedback
than did LE black males, LE black females, LE white males, and UE white
and black males. UE black females received less feedback than did LE
black males, LE black females, LE white males, and UE black and white
males.

Academic Feedback

For the combined categories of academic feedback, there was a significant interaction for gender and grade level. In the upper elementary grades, females received significantly less academic feedback than did males.

Nonacademic Feedback

There was a significant main effect for the gender factor for the nonacademic feedback statements and for the factor grade level. Males received more nonacademic feedback than did females, and LE students received more than did UE students.

Positive Student Initiating Behaviors

The results of the analysis for student initiating behavior yielded a significant effect for gender. Males initiated more positive interactions with teachers than did female students.

Negative Student Initiating Behaviors

There was a significant effect for gender for negative student initiating behaviors. Male students initiated more negative interactions with teachers than did female students.

Response Opportunities

The analysis of response opportunities resulted in a significant interaction. UE black females were provided fewer opportunities to respond in the classroom than were LE black females.

The findings in this study support the findings of earlier work on the obscurity of females in teacher-student interactions in classrooms (Brophy & Good, 1974; Cooper & Good, 1983; Leinhardt, Seewald, & Engel, 1979). This study, however, suggests more complex findings. The race of the student and the grade level of the student are important variables that influence the classroom interactions involving male and female students.

Quantitative Analysis of Teacher Feedback

Quantitatively (as defined by the total number of interactions), white females in the lower and the upper elementary grades received significantly less teacher feedback than did students in the other gender/race categories. At the lower elementary level, they received fewer teacher feedback statements than LE and UE white males, LE and UE black males, and LE black females. UE white females received significantly less teacher feedback than did LE and UE white males, LE and UE black males, and LE black females.

The quantitative profile for black females presents a more complex finding. These findings suggest that the inconspicuousness of black females in the classroom begins in the upper elementary grades, not in the lower grades, as is true for their white female counterparts. It was at the upper elementary level that black females in this study received less feedback from teachers than did LE and UE white males and LE and UE black males. In addition, UE black females received significantly less feedback than did black females in the lower grades.

These findings on the different nature of the quantitative feedback for white and black females seem to support Lewis's (1975) assertion that the early sex role socialization for black females is dissimilar from the sex role socialization of white females. Lewis concluded that blacks tended to be less sex-typed and more egalitarian about the roles of males and females than were white persons. Her description of the sex-role socialization of black families emphasized that unlike white children, black children are not inculcated with standards that polarize behavioral expectations according to sex. Sarah Lawrence Lightfoot (1976) commented that as a result of this nontraditional socialization, the black female in the classroom is likely "to be seen as assertive and bossy, rather than submissive and cuddly," as white females are perceived.

The data from this research support the early salience of black females in the lower elementary grades but suggest that teachers and schools have a significant influence in socializing black females to traditional female behaviors. By the time black females enter the upper elementary grades, they seem to have joined their white female counterparts in their invisibility, thereby resulting in fewer interactions with teachers.

Analysis of Teacher Feedback

The analysis of the differences by gender, race, and grade level of students revealed additional findings. The significant second-order interaction for the variable positive feedback resulted because LE and UE white females received less positive feedback than did UE black males. As was found for the total feedback category, UE black females experienced a significant decrease in positive feedback, receiving less than LE white males and UE black males. Interestingly, black males received more positive feedback in the UE level than in the LE level. The opposite is true for black females.

The other variable that indicates qualitative differences in feedback is the negative teacher feedback category. Male students received significantly more negative feedback statements than did female students.

The finding that males also received more nonacademic (procedural and behavioral) feedback than did females is particularly relevant when attempting to understand male salience in the classroom. The negative, nonacademic nature of their interactions seems to provide some indication as to how males command a disproportionate share of teacher communications. Brophy and Evertson's (1981) work and the studies of Datta, Schaefer, and Davis (1968), Dweck and Bush (1976), and Felsenthal (1970) support these findings. The analyses of data for nonacademic feedback also revealed that students in the lower elementary grades received less feedback than did students in the upper elementary grades. This finding seems to confirm the socializing role of lower elementary teachers in conditioning students to exhibit appropriate student behaviors. These nonacademic statements, both procedural and behavioral, decrease in the upper elementary grades as students learn appropriate institutional behaviors.

The interaction for gender and grade for the academic feedback variable revealed that in the upper elementary grades females received significantly less academic feedback than did males. The decline in academic feedback to females may be related to a phenomenon identified in studies by Crandall, Katkovsky, and Crandall (1965) and Dweck and Bush (1976); these researchers found that girls tend to excel more than boys in the lower grades, but by the time they reach junior high school, the trend reverses. Perhaps the decline in academic feedback contributes to the fact that older girls do not value achievement in school (Hutt, 1979) and contributes to their self-derogatory perception of failure (Nicholls, 1975). Limited academic feedback to older girls has been found by Hutt and Nicholls to be related to the older girls' tendency to lower their expectations and downgrade their abilities.

Student Initiating Behaviors

Although it is clear that student behaviors influence teacher behaviors, it is not clear, according to Safilios-Rothschild's (1979) review of the literature, "whether it is initially the teachers' sex-differentiated behaviors that account for and reinforce the students' sex-differentiated behaviors, or vice versa" (p. 77). The findings in this study indicate that male students initiate more positive and negative interactions than do female students. These interactions result in more contact with and verbal feedback from the teacher and provide some information about male prominence in the classroom. Brophy and Good (1974) speculated that high-achieving males assert themselves through positive initiating behaviors (i.e., dominating class discussions by answering questions without being recognized). Low-achieving males initiate through more negative behaviors, such as misbehaving and violating rules and norms. Nevertheless, high- and low-achieving males seem to demand recognition and acknowledgment by the teacher. The teacher responds reactively by giving disproportionate feedback to males.

Public Response Opportunities

A significant second-order interaction was shown for public response opportunities. UE black females were provided fewer opportunities to respond in the classroom than were LE black females. This pattern of decline for black females from LE to UE is similar to the pattern established in two other variables in this study—total communication and positive teacher feedback.

However, the variable concerning available opportunities to respond is particularly crucial and may be partially instructive as to how the decline in black females' salience in the classroom occurs. Teachers in this study (white females) may have been reacting to the cross-sex-typed behavior of black females in the lower grades and attempting at the upper level to socialize and condition black females to the traditional institutional sex role by not providing them opportunities to respond publicly in the class. Another likely possibility is that teachers become passively indifferent to black females in the upper elementary grades—not noticed or thought of as much as others. This profile is suggestive of Silberman's (1969) indifference group—students who received few response opportunities, had low rates of interaction with the teacher, were passive in the classroom, and initiated few contacts with the teachers. Brophy and Good (1974) concluded:

> The teachers were not critical or rejective toward "indifference" students; they were merely indifferent toward them. Their tendencies not to call on these students often and not to seek out as many contacts with them as with their classmates appeared to result from a failure to think about or perhaps to notice these students rather than from a

tendency to avoid them because of feelings of rejection or hostility (p. 141).

DIFFERENCES IN THE SCHOOL EXPERIENCES OF BLACK MALES AND BLACK FEMALES

Black Females

The findings in this study showed that black females in the upper elementary grades received significantly less total teacher feedback, less positive feedback, and fewer public response opportunities than did black females in the lower elementary grades. This pattern across the three different interaction variables did not occur for any other gender/race category. Black female students presented an active, interacting, and initiating profile in the early grades but joined their white female counterparts in the later grades in what seemed to be traditional female sex role behaviors.

Smith (1982), in a review of the literature, reported that black females do have different school experiences. Academically, they tend to outperform their black male counterparts and have higher career aspirations in high school. Despite their better academic performance, black females, like their white female counterparts, still perceive themselves more negatively than do black males on variables such as peer self-esteem, social abilities, and general anxiety (Hare & Castenell, 1985). What types of teacher and peer relationships do black females and black males experience in schools? Do these relationships change over time?

Black females—the lower elementary grades. A series of studies yields a set of generalizations about black female experiences in the early elementary grades (Byalick & Bersoff, 1974; Damico & Scott, 1985; Grant, 1984; Grant, 1985; Grant, 1986).

Young black girls

- receive less positive feedback than other gender/race groups
- promote compliance among classmates by enforcing teacher rules
- retaliate verbally or physically, when confronted
- are asked by teachers to help classmates with nonacademic tasks, compared with white females, who assist classmates with academic tasks

- develop social rather than academic skills and are praised by teachers for these social skills
- encounter more verbal hostility than white females do
- are more apt to fight
- are more likely to be ignored by teachers
- are less likely to be praised by teachers, who reserve praise for white females
- play a go-between role for teachers
- are more likely to interact with teachers in brief, task-related contacts, often on behalf of their peers
- are sole victims of white male students' racist remarks
- are more likely to be rebuffed by teachers when seeking attention

Black females—the upper elementary grades. Another set of generalizations applies to black girls in the upper elementary grades (Grant, 1986; Irvine, 1986).
Black girls

- tend to isolate themselves with other black females (only high-achieving black females tend to associate with white females)
- are subject to the attempts of black and white males to force them into periphery service roles
- rarely initiate conflicts but do not shy away from them
- receive fewer feedback statements than any other gender/race group
- receive fewer positive feedback statements
- receive fewer response opportunities in classes

Black females—junior high years (Bennett, 1980; Damico & Scott, 1985). At this age, black females

- continue to receive less academically oriented reinforcement from teachers
- become invisible, rarely interacting with teachers or peers
- are more likely to work alone
- receive more negative and procedural interaction
- are left out of friendship networks

Black Males

Another study by Irvine (1985) revealed that the accuracy and the stability of teacher expectations for black males differ considerably in comparison with the other gender/race categories. During the second, tenth, and final weeks of the 1983–1984 school year, nine teachers who taught fifth, sixth, and seventh grades in a large metropolitan school were asked to rank their students according to their perceptions of the students' general (global) academic ability. For the first ranking, teachers had no standardized test data or cumulative folder information concerning the students' past performance. During the tenth and final weeks of school, teachers were again asked to rank students. The student sample included 213 students—56 percent black, 44 percent white; 51 percent male, 49 percent female.

Thirty-four percent of the students were ranked by their homeroom/social studies teacher; 44 percent by their homeroom/language arts teacher; and 22 percent by their homeroom/science teacher. Of the sample, 30 percent were enrolled in the fifth grade, 37 percent in the sixth grade, and 33 percent in the seventh grade.

At the end of the school year, the California Achievement Test (CAT) scores were collected for each student. Correlations for the total sample and for subsamples of each of the four gender/race categories were analyzed for the following variables: second-week rankings with tenth-week rankings; second-week rankings with end-of-year rankings; tenth-week rankings with end-of-year rankings; second-week rankings with CAT scores; tenth-week rankings with CAT scores; and end-of-year rankings with CAT scores.

Correlation coefficients used to examine the relationship between teachers' rankings and the rankings for the total samples were moderately high. Correlations between CAT scores and second-week, tenth-week, and end-of-the-year rankings were .60, .65, and .69. However, individual teachers' correlations varied considerably—from a high correlation of .92 to a low correlation of .11. These data indicate that teachers are moderately accurate in ranking students in relationship to their standardized test scores. However, some teachers are more accurate than others in judging children's achievement levels. For one teacher in the study, the correlation between the second-week ranking and the CAT scores for all her students was .11. By the end of the year, the correlation had increased to .56. On the other hand, another teacher maintained high correlations (.91, .92, and .89) throughout the school year. These differences in the teachers' ability to perceive students accurately are an area in which much inquiry is needed.

Were there differences in the correlations of teacher rankings and CAT scores for each of the four gender/race categories? For white male and black male students, the relationship between rankings and standardized test scores was high for the second week (.63 and .62, respectively). By the tenth week of school, the situation changed dramatically. White males were being perceived more accurately in relationship to their test scores; black males were perceived less accurately. The correlation coefficients for black males increased by the end of the year, but the profile for the black males is quite different from the profile of white males because the teachers perceived white males' potential more accurately and over time more accurately judged their ability.

Once teachers make an initial assessment of a student, is this assessment likely to change over time? For all students, not considering sex and race, the correlations between second-week rankings and tenth-week rankings, between second-week and end-of-year rankings, and between tenth-week and end-of-year rankings are high and significant.

When the gender and race of the students were taken into consideration, it seemed that by the second week of school, teachers had firm impressions of males, particularly black males, and that these impressions remained unchanged throughout the school year. Teachers were more likely to be flexible in reevaluating their rankings of black and white females. However, by the tenth week, teachers had well-formed expectations of all their students that remained unaltered throughout the remainder of the year. The primacy effect seems operative here. That is, once teachers form an initial impression of a student, that impression is likely to remain stable.

The significance of the finding that teachers form stable, unchanging, and often inaccurate achievement expectations, in particular about black males, is of concern to educators. It may be that teachers' expectations for black males' achievement are more influenced by their stereotypes of black males as potential disruptors than by their academic ability.

Black males—the lower elementary grades (Coates, 1972; Eaves, 1975; Grant, 1986; Irvine, 1985; Simpson & Erickson, 1983; Taylor, 1979). Young black males are

- more likely to interact with other black males and least likely to interact with the teacher
- more likely to have nonacademic interactions with peers
- more likely to use a cooperative learning style

- more likely to receive controlling statements and qualified praise
- more likely to be labeled deviant and described more negatively than white males
- less likely to receive positive feedback
- more likely to receive nonverbal criticism

Black males—the upper elementary/junior high years (Grant, 1986; Irvine, 1986). Black males are

- more likely to be in the lowest academic track
- more likely to be isolated socially and academically from white students
- more likely than white males to be sent to the principal's office for challenging the teacher
- more likely to be judged inaccurately by teachers

Bruce Hare (Hare and Castenell, 1985) has referred to black males as the "endangered species" because, compared to other gender-race groups, they have the highest dropout, suspension, and expulsion rates, the highest rate of infant mortality, and the shortest life expectancy, and they are more likely to be unemployed, underemployed, or incarcerated. After researching the status of five hundred fifth-grade black boys, Hare concluded, "Put simply, black males are probably the most feared, least likely to be identified with, and least likely to be effectively taught" (p. 211).

Black males have lower standardized achievement scores, lower school self-esteem, and less achievement orientation then do black females. In a fourteen-year study by Schiamberg (1986), 50 percent of the black boys as middle school students aspired to professional and technical jobs, but in a follow-up, only 7 percent were working in such jobs. Fewer white males as middle school students aspired to these jobs, but eventually more were employed in them.

The New Orleans school system discovered that although black males represented 43 percent of the 1986–1987 school population, they accounted for 58 percent of the nonpromotions, 65 percent of the suspensions, 80 percent of expulsions, 45 percent of dropouts, and only 19 percent of gifted students. The report (Garibaldi, 1988) described the educational performance of black males as "a crisis of epidemic proportions" (p. 2).

The cumulative effects of black males' lack of school achievement are reflected in the number who matriculate and graduate from institutions of higher education. Data from the Department of Education for 1984 ("Racial and Ethnic Makeup," 1986) indicated that 200,000 more black women than black men were enrolled in institutions of higher education. Black women undergraduates outnumbered black male undergraduates by more than 160,000.

Any consideration of the school experiences of black children must take into account the gender of the children. It seems nonproductive to posit that black males are more at risk than black females, or vice versa. What is pertinent is that both groups, for different reasons, experience discrimination and isolation with a similar outcome—poor academic achievement.

APPENDIX: DESCRIPTION OF METHODOLOGY FOR CHAPTER 4

METHOD

Unit of Analysis

The unit of analysis was a communication interaction that was obtained in 1983 from sixty-three classrooms in ten schools in four public school systems in the Southeast. Of the 1,706 communication interactions coded, 53 percent were collected in a standard metropolitan statistical area school system, and 47 percent were collected from three rural school systems. Grade levels included kindergarten through fifth grade, with the majority of the data (59 percent) collected in grades K–2 and 41 percent in grades 3–5. There were fifty-eight white teachers and five black teachers, all of whom were females. The classrooms observed were homogeneous (average ability) and self-contained. The subject matter taught during the observations varied. Most lessons (76 percent) were in language arts; 15 percent were mathematics lessons; and the remainder of the observations were conducted during science or social studies classes. There were 1,328 children present in the sixty-three classrooms observed: 430 white males, 311 white females, 296 black males, and 291 black females. Each of the sixty-three classes was observed once during a three-week period. No student or teacher was observed in a classroom more than once.

Observers

Three observers participated in the study—one black female, one white female, and one black male. The observers received a total of forty hours of training by videotaped classroom instruction and in-school observations. The interobserver agreement ranged from 0.80 to 1.0.

Data Collection

The teachers who participated in this study were not told the purpose of the study. A data collector went to the classroom at the beginning of each class and sat in an unobtrusive position at the side of the class, near the middle. The mean time of observation in the sixty-three classes was forty minutes, and the mean number of children present during observations was twenty.

INSTRUMENTATION

Teacher Verbal Feedback Statements

The instrument used was the author's modification of the Brophy-Good Dyadic Interaction System (Good and Brophy, 1978). The modified instrument was adopted because its feedback categories yield both quantitative and qualitative data. Three major teacher feedback categories were used—positive, negative, and neutral. A fourth category, total communications, was the combination of the three major categories and represented the quantitative amount of feedback and contact between students and teachers. In addition, data were collected and analyzed according to the context of the teacher's remark—academic or nonacademic. Categories were operationally defined as follows:

1. *Positive* statements included statements of praise and affirmations of correct responses. Praise statements expressed strong teacher affect and enhanced the student's status in the classroom. Examples included statements such as "Fine!," "Great!," "I'm so proud of you!," and "That's a terrific answer!" Affirmations of correct responses were indications that the students' responses were correct. Examples of such responses were "OK," "All right," "Yes," and "Correct."

2. *Negative* statements included statements of criticism and negation of incorrect responses. Critical statements referred to expressions of disapproval and rejection or prohibitory messages. Examples of criticism were "Can't you do any better?" and "That's a ridiculous answer." Statements of negation included "No," "That's wrong," and "Incorrect."

3. *Neutral* statements were not critical, affirming, or praising. The teacher's routine repetition of a student's answer, the teacher's procedural statements, and the teacher's related questions or responses to a student's answer were typical of the statements in this category. Such statements included "Does 7 x 5 = 30?," "Is that right?," "Are you listening?," "Be careful," "Read on," and "Go get the crayons."

4. *Total Communication* was a combination of the first three categories and was a quantitative representation of the feedback given to students.

5. *Academic Communication* was related to instruction and subject matter concerns.

6. *Nonacademic Communication* was related to a behavioral or a procedural context. A behavioral communication referred to a student's conduct or deportment; a procedural statement was related to the giving of directions, requests for supplies and materials, and specifications about routine classroom managerial matters.

Student Initiating Behaviors

When a student initiated an interaction, the student's behavior was coded as positive or negative.

1. *Positive* initiating behaviors included such acts as raising one's hand to respond to a teacher's question or request, volunteering to participate in an assignment or to perform a classroom responsibility, or calling out an answer and having the response accepted by the teacher.

2. *Negative* initiating behaviors included some clear violation of classroom rules or norms that resulted in a negative response by the teacher and a student's calling out an answer and having the response rejected by the teacher.

Public Response Opportunities

A public response opportunity represents the number of opportunities that students have to respond in the classroom as a result of the teacher's calling on a nonvolunteering student or as a result of the teacher's calling a student's name before asking the question.

Experimental Design

The raw data for each category of teacher feedback, student initiating behaviors, and response opportunities were classified according to student gender and race and transformed into scores based on the group's representation within each classroom (Hillman & Davenport, 1978; Simpson & Erickson, 1983). The following formula was used:

$$\frac{\text{Total number of interactions for variable in a given student's gender/race category}}{\text{Total number of interactions for a variable}} \times \frac{\text{Total number of students in classroom}}{\text{Total number of students in gender/race category}}$$

A score represents the proportion of the expected share of the feedback that was received by a gender/race category. A proportional score of 1 for a gender/race category means that the students in that particular category received their expected share of interactions. Scores more than or less than 1 indicate the proportion of the expected share of interactions that was actually observed.

Proportional share scores for the dependent variables were analyzed in relation to the student's gender (male, female), student's race (black, white), and student's grade level (lower elementary [K–2] and upper elementary [3–5]). The three-way factorial analyses of variance (ANOVA) procedure of the Statistical Package for the Social Sciences (Nie et al., 1975) was used to analyze the data. The a posteriori test used to evaluate all pairwise comparisons was the Modified Least Significant Difference Test (MLSD).

RESULTS

Table A.1 presents the means and standard deviations for the nine communication variables for each gender/race category for each of the two grade levels. The results of the nine three-way analyses of variance are shown in Table A.2. The ANOVAs reveal four significant main effects for gender (negative, nonacademic, positive student initiating, negative student initiating); no significant main effects for race; one significant main effect for grade level (nonacademic); one significant first-order interaction (academic); and three significant second-order interactions (positive feedback, total communications, response opportunity).

Table A.1
Average Proportional Shares for Each Sex/Race Category

| | Grade K - 2 | | | | Grade 3 - 5 | | | |
| | White | | Black | | White | | Black | |
Sex	X̄	(S.D.)	X̄	(S.D.)	X̄	(S.D.)	X̄	(S.D.)
	N = 34		N = 37		N = 20		N = 19	
	N = 35		N = 36		N = 21		N = 22	
Positive teacher feedback								
Males	1.22	(1.05)	0.69	(0.66)	1.11	(0.72)	1.45	(1.95)
Females	0.79	(0.64)	1.03	(0.93)	0.70	(0.62)	0.60	(0.61)
Neutral teacher feedback								
Males	0.90	(0.73)	0.80	(1.01)	0.81	(0.68)	0.76	(0.54)
Females	0.52	(0.53)	0.94	(0.94)	0.42	(0.58)	0.53	(0.61)
Negative teacher feedback								
Males	0.48	(0.55)	0.55	(0.52)	0.49	(0.53)	0.48	(0.57)
Females	0.16	(0.31)	0.41	(0.55)	0.32	(0.49)	0.23	(0.31)
Total communications								
Males	0.76	(0.47)	0.66	(0.38)	0.72	(0.43)	0.76	(0.55)
Females	0.40	(0.30)	0.72	(0.44)	0.43	(0.32)	0.41	(0.31)
Academic communications								
Males	0.93	(0.70)	0.68	(0.53)	1.03	(0.70)	1.08	(0.97)
Females	0.67	(0.57)	0.94	(0.68)	0.82	(0.55)	0.60	(0.55)
Nonacademic								
Males	0.80	(0.79)	0.75	(1.06)	0.54	(0.62)	0.58	(0.60)
Females	0.20	(0.40)	0.65	(0.86)	0.07	(0.25)	0.26	(0.59)
Positive Student Initiating Behavior								
Males	1.02	(1.22)	0.86	(1.45)	0.78	(1.06)	1.07	(1.67)
Females	0.52	(0.83)	0.97	(1.59)	0.25	(0.45)	0.41	(0.94)
Negative Student Initiating								
Males	1.13	(1.14)	1.19	(1.75)	1.01	(1.17)	0.87	(1.18)
Females	0.37	(0.87)	0.67	(1.07)	0.47	(1.27)	0.34	(0.73)
Public Response Opportunities								
Males	1.18	(0.51)	1.12	(0.96)	1.06	(0.51)	1.24	(0.90)
Females	0.87	(0.72)	1.28	(1.19)	1.07	(0.54)	0.70	(0.44)

Table A.2
Analysis of Variance for Communication Variables as a Function of Student Sex, Race, and Grade Level

Variable	Sex (S)	Race (R)	Grade level (GL)	S X R	S X GL	R X GL	S X R X GL	Error
Positive teacher feedback								
MS	3.500	0.172	0.028	1.499	4.533	0.843	4.759	0.839
F	3.953*	0.193	0.032	1.685	5.119*	0.948	5.351*	
Neutral teacher feedback								
MS	1.901	0.711	1.318	2.047	0.469	0.228	0.412	0.579
F	3.285	1.229	2.277	3.537	0.810	0.394	0.712	
Negative teacher feedback								
MS	2.776	0.396	0.017	0.110	0.002	0.633	0.242	0.243
F	11.407**	1.627	0.071	1.002	0.006	2.601	0.995	
Total communications								
MS	2.557	0.268	0.200	0.798	0.383	0.136	0.729	0.168
F	15.246**	1.596	1.190	4.759*	2.287	0.809	4.347*	
Academic communications								
MS	1.114	0.010	0.104	0.984	2.031	0.047	1.472	0.434
F	2.567	0.024	0.240	2.268	4.679*	0.108	3.392	
Nonacademic communications								
MS	7.330	1.613	2.923	1.807	0.025	0.113	0.387	0.534
F	13.724**	3.021	5.472*	3.384	0.047	0.212	0.725	
Positive student initiating								
MS	6.391	1.635	2.504	1.585	2.120	0.065	1.734	1.540
F	4.149	1.061	1.626	1.029	1.377	0.042	1.126	
Negative student initiating								
MS	20.387	0.261	1.443	0.333	0.149	1.332	0.178	1.457
F	13.966**	0.179	0.991	0.228	0.102	0.914	0.122	
Public Response opportunities								
MS	1.156	0.292	0.523	0.120	0.497	1.022	3.293	0.654
F	1.797	0.454	0.813	0.186	0.773	1.589	5.177*	

Note. MS refers to significant main effect; F refers to four interactions. dfs = 1 for each main effect and interaction, df = 216 for error.

*p < .05
**p < .001

5

Effective Strategies for Committed Educators

> We can, whenever and wherever we choose, successfully teach all children whose schooling is of interest to us. We already know more than we need to do that. Whether or not we do it must finally depend on how we feel about the fact that we haven't so far.
>
> Ronald Edmonds,
> *Educational Leadership*,
> p. 23.

This chapter reviews some strategies that are associated with enhancing and promoting the achievement of black students. Its focus is on identifying methods that can potentially increase the school achievement of black students by decreasing the hidden conflict that results from lack of cultural synchronization and increasing the expectations of teachers, schools, and parents. However, it must be emphasized that the continuing cycle of failure for black students is not directly related to a lack of informed and prudent strategies for remediation. Many individuals as well as organizations continue to devote their professional careers to finding and implementing such strategies. (See Slavin, Karweit, & Madden [1989] for descriptions of effective instructional programs.) The modest success of these methods, programs, and strategies consistently to enhance black students' achievement has more to do with the lack of a long-range, visionary national policy on minority youth than with the attributes of any particular strategy or program. Addressing the educational needs of black students in the absence of a national policy that serves as a framework for guided decision making and experimentation has resulted in some predictable outcomes—lack of coordination of efforts, ill-conceived and poorly executed myopic projects, and eventual abandonment by short-sighted, politically motivated individuals.

In addition to the lack of a national policy, there is a scarcity of committed practitioners and policymakers who are willing to tackle the problem of black students' nonachievement from a historical perspective—recognizing that educational planning for an oppressed and previously enslaved people requires more than short-lived interventions. The lack of generational human resolve is the factor that continues the cycle of reinventing the proverbial wheel.

The strategies described in this chapter are intended to be not exhaustive, but representative of some of the types of remedies that seem related to black students' school achievement, provided there are the requisite leadership, a national policy, a cadre of committed and informed educators, a system for providing rewards for educators, and a staff development program that focuses on professional development, training, and organizational renewal.

It must also be noted that many of the recommendations have been treated extensively in the educational literature and that some apply generally to all students, not just black or minority students. Although some of these instructional interventions are helpful to majority students, their successful implementation are imperative and critically important for underachieving black students.

The strategies are organized by four different perspectives—the Afrocentric instructional research, the teaching effectiveness research, the effective schools research, and the parental involvement research.

AFROCENTRIC RESEARCH

This school of thought addresses the lack of achievement of black students from the perspective that schools are not culturally responsive (and in some instances are overtly racist) to children of Afro-American heritage. The remedies proposed by Janice Hale-Benson, A. Wade Boykin, the National Alliance of Black School Educators, David Houlton, Godfrey L. Brandt, and Wilma S. Longstreet adopt this perspective.

Hale-Benson's (1986) prescriptions focus on the implementation of a curriculum that is "relevant to Afro-Americans" (p. 151). Her educational philosophy centers around political/cultural ideology, pedagogical relevance, and academic rigor. The ideological base for this remedy posits that schools, as they presently exist, cooperate with other institutions in the economic and political oppression of black people and that any relevant curriculum for black children must have as its foundation consciousness-raising for struggle and eventual liberation.

The goal of the Hale-Benson curriculum is to help children learn through experiences that are both Afro- and Euro-American—such as language/communication skills, mathematical concepts, and Afro-American studies. In addition, Hale-Benson includes affective goals—in other words, the development of positive attitudes toward self, learning, and school. Other distinctive features of the Hale-Benson program include strategies such as chanting, storytelling, frequent touching and hugging, frequent physical movement in both play and learning activities, group rather than individual learning, and the use of Afro-American music as a method to relax and discipline black children.

Boykin (1986) and other researchers (Cureton, 1978; Slaughter, 1969) believe that black children achieve in a curriculum that capitalizes on their cultural learning style. This cultural learning style is characterized by activities involving physical movement. Boykin noticed that black homes accommodate large numbers of family members. Consequently, they are usually noisy, stimulating, and centered around activities that involve physical movement. In his own experiments, he found that the performance of black children was enhanced when teachers employed a variety of activities with "verve inducement and high sensate stimulation" (p. 6). Boykin, like Hale-Benson (1986), believes that learning activities that require physical movements such as dancing and hand clapping contribute to black students' achievement. Cureton (1978) also thinks that oral involvement is beneficial, particularly oral involvement that emphasizes familiar group recitations and choral responses.

The National Alliance of Black School Educators (NABSE) emphatically states in a 1984 report that one of the primary barriers to black students' achievement is racism. Hence, their organizational ideology asserts that the cumulative and the historical effects of racism must be rectified through equity, academic excellence, and cultural relevance. The proposed program of NABSE gives attention to the study of the history and the cultural heritage of African Americans. NABSE believes that

to a large degree, the negative attitudes and reactions which many European Americans have toward African Americans are shaped by the sins of omission and commission that are operative in public education's treatment of African and African-American history and culture (p. 23).

A performance-based curriculum is proposed by NABSE, with courses in mathematics (algebra in sixth grade, calculus in the twelfth), economics, political science, computer competence, history, language arts, foreign language (with an African language as an option), sciences, vocational education, and African-American history and culture. Also recommended for black students is the teaching of critical thinking skills, creativity, and problem solving. In conjunction with this curriculum, NABSE has proposed an Institute for African American Education, which will develop culturally relevant educational materials as well as train teachers and administrators to be sensitive to the needs of black students. Presently, the Council of Independent Black Institutions (Lomotey & Brookins, 1988) offers a training institute for persons interested in Afrocentric schools.

Brandt (1986), in his book *The Realization of Anti-Racist Teaching*, describes how sensitivity toward minority children can be achieved by directly addressing the issue of racism in classrooms. His specific recommendations for addressing racism are crucial elements that are missing from both the Hale-Benson and the NABSE works. Brandt states that the goal of antiracist teaching is "to oppose whatever operates to oppress, repress, or disenfranchise one set of people" (p. 125) and to address any assumptions that white persons are inherently superior to persons of color. He offers a prescription for antiracist teaching that embraces equality and works actively to deconstruct all systems and structures that foster and perpetuate racism. Other goals of antiracist teaching are justice and the liberation of the oppressed and the oppressor.

Brandt's recommends that teachers be trained in the nature of racism and racial suppression in educational institutions. In the classroom, he favors the elimination of didactic and individual approaches to instruction in favor of collaborative, group-centered learning. In these collaborative classrooms, the teacher is not a lecturer but a consultant, arbitrator, facilitator, and provoker who critically analyzes racist curricula in an effort to design an antiracist one that challenges racism, sexism, and classism.

Houlton's research (1986) is complementary to Brandt's. He notes that cultural diversity in the classroom is improved when teachers, primarily, establish a welcoming ethos that provides children with an opportunity to speak freely, learn collaboratively, and incorporate their out-of-school experiences into the classroom. In addition, cultural diversity is established through the constant use of multicultural visual materials in the classroom; the valuing of the children's and their parents' knowledge, skills, and experiences; the open and critical discussion of race and racism; and a curriculum that is multicultural and multilingual.

Afrocentric responses to instruction have little support in traditional public and private schools. School personnel have not been willing to pilot these strategies, preferring instead basic instructional techniques of drill and practice, mastery learning, and the performance-based curriculum.

Black parents have in the past been reluctant to endorse innovative curricula and instead have preferred conservative and traditional schools. Lightfoot (1978) conjectured that black parents feel that their children receive an inferior education if it does not resemble their perceptions of white children's schooling. It seems that the advocates of these culturally specific recommendations have to develop first a strong community base of support. There also has to be an acknowledgment that the majority of black children will continue to attend Eurocentric public schools, which resist change of any type, especially when there are few, if any, incentives offered to do so.

Another concern is the lack of an empirical base to support some Afrocentric prescriptions. For example, does the lack of variety in learning activities and methods, as well as lack of physical movement, negatively impact black children more than their white peers? In his seminal work, *A Place Called School*, Goodlad (1984) observed over one thousand classes and found that 60 percent of class time in elementary school was spent doing the following: preparing for and cleaning up after assignments, listening to teachers explain or lecture, and carrying out written assignments. In addition, 6 percent of the time was spent taking quizzes and nearly 8 percent on off-task behaviors. The average class was left with only 25 percent for other types of activities.

What Goodlad and others found was lack of instructional variability for most children regardless of race. Seldom (except in art, music, and physical education) were children being taught with methods involving physical movement, varied methods, or high affect. Unfortunately, what researchers now understand about classroom teaching is that teachers actually use a very limited repertoire of pedagogical methods: they talk or monitor seat work. "Teacher talk" is usually lecturing, giving directions, or asking questions. The seat work is the infamous routine of students' reading dittos and completing short answer or multiple-choice questions. The order of the day is to set contingencies in which there are minimal student movement, minimal student-to-student interaction, minimal student-to-teacher interaction, and minimal intimate affect.

If this scenario is descriptive of the majority of our schools, then it seems fair to speculate that this dismal situation is intensified in schools that serve black children. In these schools, the overwhelming preoccupation seems to be with control—particularly controlling the physical movement and anticipated and perceived aggression of black male children. Given these conditions, all children, particularly black children, would welcome "verve inducement" in these classrooms.

More systematic empirical study of the relationship between black culture and school achievement, specifically cultural discontinuity, is needed. How can this relationship be empirically investigated? Longstreet's (1978) structure for studying aspects of ethnicity provides a framework for such an investigation. She describes in detail five aspects of ethnicity: verbal communication, nonverbal communication, orientation modes, social value patterns, and intellectual modes.

Black verbal or oral communication can be studied from the standpoint of its grammatical structure, semantic structure involving denotations and connotations, and phonological structure (sound formation, pausal behavior, tempo, rhythm, pitch). Discussion modes are also important aspects of verbal language. Discussions can be informative, controversial, exploratory, playful, or insulting. This aspect of Afro-American culture has received the most attention from scholars, and Chapter 2 of this book summarizes that body of literature.

Nonverbal communications involve movements of the body and physical space to transmit or receive messages. Kinesics is the study of nonverbal communications based on body movements; the work by Cooke (1972) is one of the first essays on the subject of black nonverbal language. Proxemics is the study of interpersonal space. Longstreet says that one's personality, as well as culture, influences perceptions of personal space. Black students often state that some white teachers physically position themselves too close, causing some black students to become anxious and uncomfortable. It is also common for black students obtrusively to invade the personal space of another black student in order to provoke a confrontation. Other forms of nonverbal communications include haptics (the study of interpersonal touching), symbols, and signals. More research related specifically to this area of communication is needed.

Orientation modes include body orientations, attention modes, and time modes. Black students' body orientations and body stances were also studied by Cooke (1972), who identified several body orientations and the meanings associated with them—stances for pimping, rapping, conversing, woofing. An important area of investigation is the way attention spans are related to culture and ethnicity. Black students are often characterized as having short attention spans, hence the recommendations for frequent varied activities and physical movement. A standard commentary in the black community is that black people have a different orientation to time; that is, blacks are frequently "late," and whites are sometimes annoyed or perplexed. Is there empirical evidence for this speculation? How does this difference in time orientation affect black students' success in school? Since standardized tests are timed, could this factor have a bearing on the results obtained? A recent study (Rosser, 1989) indicated that blacks take longer to complete the verbal section of the SAT, possibly contributing to their lower test scores.

The study of social value patterns assumes that every ethnic group has a set of social practices and behaviors and that all members are expected to comply with them. Cultural deficit theorists posit that these cultural expectations for blacks are dysfunctional and often pathological, contributing to failure in school, leaving school, poverty, and a life of frequent crime. A social value among black youth, according to Fordham and Ogbu (1986), is the equation of successful school achievement with "acting white." This social value portends that black students who achieve in school are denying their racial identity and acting white. Examples of other social values and behaviors by black youth include athletic and dance abilities, a sense of humor, and the ability to use words rhythmically.

Finally, Longstreet discusses intellectual modes of cognition, a topic covered in Chapter 2. Obviously, much school research is needed on this complex topic. Do black students organize information differently from white students? How, for instance, are reasoning, both spatial and abstract, and verbal fluency influenced by culture?

In summary, Afrocentric instructional responses attempt to identify the distinctive cultural retentions of black students and to develop teaching strategies that are compatible with them. This line of inquiry is in its infancy, and more research is needed. Of particular concern is the seeming dissonance between Afrocentric techniques of instruction and the wishes of black parents to have their children taught in traditional schools and with traditional instructional strategies.

RELEVANT FINDINGS FROM TEACHING EFFECTIVENESS RESEARCH

A second school of thought aimed at effectively teaching black and minority students is grounded in teaching effectiveness research. The teacher effectiveness research movement is nearly nine decades old. Researchers' interest in identifying the characteristics of good teaching has not subsided, and it continues to be an active area of inquiry. Recently, longitudinal data from compensatory programs in the sixties and seventies have produced strong findings related to the effective teaching of at-risk children. Certainly, good teaching benefits all students' learning, but underachieving black students need to be taught by teachers recognized as effective and experienced. Brophy (1982), Hawley et al. (1984), and

Cruickshank (1985) summarized these findings in their reviews of the literature.

Effective teachers of minority children have high expectations for their students. These teachers do not prejudge or categorize students based solely on standardized test scores, social class, or behavior. When their pupils do not initially master the materials, these effective teachers do not ascribe blame to external factors, such as the child's parents or previous teachers, nor do they impute negative characteristics to the child. They restructure the learning activities, assuming that the child has not yet mastered the materials, not that the child is incapable or unwilling to learn. Brophy (1982) said, "If something is not learned the first time through, they teach it again" (p. 527). Like a coach, these teachers do not think of teaching as mere "coverage" of materials, but as the development of intellectual habits through practice. Wiggins (1988) stressed the point that teaching is "successive approximations perfected in cycles of model-practice-feedback, rather than one-shot didactic lessons or drills" (p. 28).

These teachers maximize learning time, concentrating on teaching academic tasks and allocating available time for instruction. Effective teachers of minority children must be excellent instructional organizers, classroom managers, and time managers. When you enter the classroom of one of these teachers, you see students who know what to do and when to do it. They know where instructional materials are located, when and how to make the transition from one lesson to the next, and how to line up and leave the classroom. Seldom will effective teachers waste time attending to routine procedures—calling the name of each student for attendance, passing papers, sharpening pencils, setting up equipment, moving furniture, or repeating directions or rules. Early in the school year, teachers make their expectations known; they consistently reward students for complying. As time passes, students are given increasing responsibility for more complex, recurring classroom practices.

Not every researcher recommends that low-income or low-achieving students be given the freedom to choose their activities or to do independent work. Some believe that low-income students "become frustrated, suffer task completion, and lower learning" from lack of structure (Hawley et al., 1984a, p. 23). Brophy (1982) stated, "Inner-city students in particular profit from structure and teacher guidance" (p. 529). That is to say, when low-income students' physical space and learning activities are not highly structured, they become frustrated and do not successfully complete their assignments. Many teachers exaggerate this point and fail to give minority and/or low-income students any freedom of movement, choice of assignments, or responsibility for routine tasks.

Minority students learn and master instructional materials when there is a match between their present achievement level and the task to be completed. The assignment should not be so difficult that the student consistently fails or so easy that the student perceives the work as meaningless or unchallenging. Supporters of Bloom's (1976) concept of mastery learning assert that students should achieve at least a 90 percent success rate. Mastery with at least an 80 percent success rate seems especially important for seat work and homework, tasks where students often work alone. Often black children complete their home assignments when adults are working or away from the home. When seat work and homework are completed without adult supervision or peer tutoring, some black students reinforce errors and develop dysfunctional study habits.

Effective teachers of minority students can be identified by their relentless levels of energy and exuberance. They move about the classroom and use their bodies, voices, and facial gestures as teaching instruments. These teachers do not shy away from touching their students—a pat on the back or a hug for a job well done. Researchers refer to this teaching technique as interactive or active. It involves acceptance of students' ideas, frequent feedback, demonstrations, explanations, questions, rephrasing, reviews, drills, recitations, monitoring, individualizing, summarizing, and reinforcing. The pace is brisk, and the activities are varied. A master teacher using these techniques with twenty-five or more eager students resembles a conductor with a symphony orchestra. A recent, longitudinal follow-up study of one thousand low-income black students in Project Follow Through (Gersten & Keating, 1987) concluded that black students who were taught interactively had lower drop-out rates and higher college attendance than black students taught by other methods.

The classrooms of successful teachers of minority children are pleasant, friendly, and open, not hostile and repressive. In repressive environments, the faces of children mirror the climate. They stare blankly at the teacher or peer out of windows in hopes of seeing something or someone interesting. These children do not smile, laugh, or behave spontaneously; frequently they doodle, spin pencils, flip through pages. Class rules (stated in the negative) are posted prominently on the walls. On the other hand, it is easy to ascertain when both teacher and students want to be with each other. The atmosphere is amicable, enthusiastic, and responsive, yet orderly at the same time. Brown (1986), in *Teaching Minorities More Effectively: A Model for Educators*, warns teachers that ignoring the inappropriate behaviors of black students leads to eventual disruption, but moralizing, demeaning, and engaging in power struggles are equally ineffective. Teachers should use positive reinforcement to change behaviors, be consistent and fair, and avoid verbal exchanges designed to berate and belittle students.

In summary, effective teachers of minority students have high expectations; optimize academic learning time; organize, manage, and plan well; match instructional objectives to the student's ability; use active teaching methods; and maintain a pleasant and respectful classroom environment.

Qualifications of the Teaching Effectiveness Research

These findings appear to be sound, logical, and related to teachers' common knowledge of "what works." However, more work in identifying the elements of effective instruction for at-risk minority students needs to be planned, implemented, and evaluated. For example, I have observed that recognized effective teachers of at-risk black children often ignore and sometimes violate the principles of effective teaching. One researcher, in a study of effective independent black schools, noted that the classrooms were not always orderly, quiet, or high on "time on task" (Lomotey & Brookins, 1988).

Jaime Escalante, depicted in the movie *Stand and Deliver*, is illustrative of this point. This Hispanic teacher achieved impressive results with the Hispanic students in an inner-city school in Los Angeles. Before Escalante came to this school, there were no advanced placement math classes; presently, this school produces one-half of all Hispanic students who pass advanced placement calculus. Escalante is representative of a teacher in cultural synchronization with his students but whose teaching behaviors often contradict the teacher effectiveness research.

In one scene in the movie, Escalante decides that his remedial students are "too smart for basic math" and starts to teach them the concept of positive and negative numbers. He uses a beach analogy, a common experience for these students. He asks one gang member, "You ever been to the beach? Every play in the sand? Dig a hole? The sand that comes out of the hole is a positive. The hole is the negative. It's simple; anybody can do. Tell me. Negative 2 and positive 2 equals?"

The gang member stares defiantly, refusing to respond. Escalante pushes and persists. The student finally mumbles, "Zero."

He uses their shared history and culture as methods to encourage and inspire. Escalante tells his Hispanic students that the Greeks and Romans were not capable of understanding zero. But their ancestors, the Mayans, invented the concept. Escalante boasts, "You burros have math in your blood!"

He tells the students that his classroom is his domain and begins to establish his credibility and establish his authority with the Hispanic male students by engaging in a verbal macho confrontation. In the black community, it is often called joning or profiling. A naive classroom observer would wrongly accuse Escalante of ridiculing and humiliating his students in his outbursts: "I'll jump on your face and tattoo your chromosomes"; "We are going to need a lot of Kleenex because there's going to be a lot of blood shed"; "I'll break your neck like a toothpick."

Mr. Escalante is obviously an excellent teacher, although some principles of the teaching effectiveness research are ignored in his classroom. The effective teaching research provides a useful framework and organizer for the instruction of at-risk, low-income black students; however, we still don't know enough about effective instructional strategies for these students.

Eliminating Tracking

A description of tracking and its negative consequences for black student achievement are treated in Chapter 1. Some alternatives to tracking or homogeneous grouping include Mortimer Adler's Paideia Proposal, Oakes's curriculum, and Slavin's cooperative learning.

The Paideia Proposal. Adler's (1982) one-track system of instruction prescribes that all students, whether they are college-bound or not, be given the same type of schooling. The Greek word *paideia* means, in fact, learning that should be acquired by all human beings. This structural change in the curriculum can provide the framework for raised teacher expectations for black students. Instead of blaming students for inequities that result from environmental factors, the Paideia Proposal recommends curriculum reform starting with one to three years of public preschool education. In addition to the preschool experience, there are twelve years of study divided into three distinct modes of teaching and learning.

Didactic instruction, using texts and lectures, is used as a method to assist students in acquiring organized knowledge about nature, man, and society. The relevant subjects for didactic instruction include (but are not limited to) language, literature, mathematics, natural science, history, geography, and social studies. In the second mode, students develop intellectual and learning skills through a method of instruction referred to as coaching, exercises, or supervised practice. Students practice and develop skills in reading, writing, speaking, listening, calculating, problem solving, observing, measuring, estimating, and critical judgment. The Maieutic or Socratic method, the third mode, is used to improve the understanding of ideas and values. Through discussion and questioning, students explore great books, music, art, and drama in an informal and collegial atmosphere. In addition to this required curriculum, students must take twelve years of physical education, basic manual skills such as cooking, sewing, and carpentry, and courses related to the world of work.

The Oakes Proposal. Oakes's (1986) solution to tracking is a simple and direct approach. She argued that "the first and most obvious way to undo the negative effects of tracking is to reorganize schools so that similar students are not grouped for instruction" (p. 151). She proposed that the curriculum be reconstructed from its present scope and sequence approach, a presentation of series of topics and skills that require prerequisite knowledge and prior mastery of skills, to a curriculum that is organized around themes and ideas. She suggests restructuring the classroom to encompass a variety of teaching methods designed to address the diverse needs of students in a heterogeneous class.

Cooperative Learning. Cooperative learning is another instructional methodology that can be used as an alternative to tracking. Cooperative learning confronts society's premise that competition fosters academic excellence and student development. Combs's (1979) and Kohn's (1986) works provide convincing arguments, supported by sociological and psychological research, to debunk the myth of the benefits of competition by referring to its negative effect on trust, tolerance, achievement, self-esteem, anxiety, security, and the formation of friendships.

One adverse effect of competition, according to Combs, is that it tends to make the people who are competing more alike. Competition can work only if people agree to seek the same goals and follow the same rules. Accordingly, as competitors strive to beat each other's records, they tend to become conformist. The benefits of competition must be assessed not only in terms of visible, concrete outcomes but also in terms of the less visible, human consequences that may in the long run be far more important.

Cooperative learning methods have been promoted primarily by Slavin (1980, 1982, 1987a, 1987b). There is substantial evidence in the literature to suggest that students achieve significantly more when they are in classrooms where they work together rather than when they are alone or in competition with each other. Most relevant are Slavin's findings that cooperative learning methods are particularly successful with black students in all-black and in desegrated schools. Perhaps there is a relationship between Slavin's conclusion and observations that black children are more relational than analytical in their learning style, preferring group-oriented rather than individual activities. (For a more detailed description refer to Chapter 2.)

Several methods have been developed by Slavin and his colleagues at Johns Hopkins University: Student Teams Achievement Divisions (STAD), Teams-Games-Tournaments (TGT), Team Accelerated Instruction (TAI), and Cooperative Integrated Reading and Composition (CIRC). These four approaches are representative of many different cooperative learning methods.

In STAD, students are assigned to four- or five-person teams composed of high-, average-, and low-ability students. Teachers are encouraged to include males and females and students of different ethnic and racial backgrounds on each team. When new materials are introduced to the class, the team decides on the method it will use to master the materials. Team members are told that they have not completed their work until each team member understands the material and is ready to be tested. Students are tested individually, and the teacher computes team scores. All teams whose scores meet or exceed a predetermined criterion receive special recognition. Because STAD focuses on improvement, every student, including low-ability students, can successfully contribute to the team effort.

Teams-Games-Tournaments (TGT) is similar to STAD, except that in TGT students compete in weekly tournaments to demonstrate mastery. Tournament tables are set up in the classroom, and a student might compete with students from other teams whose past performance and ability are similar. This system, like STAD, makes it possible for all students to contribute to the team score.

Team Accelerated Instruction (TAI) is a combination of team and individual instruction with a focus on the teaching of mathematics. A diagnostic test determines the appropriate level of instruction for the student who completes a set of programmed materials. Team members check each other's work. When a student passes with a score of 80 percent or better, a final test is given and scored by a student monitor. Students' test scores and the number of tests completed in a week comprise the team score. Because students check each other's work and monitor tests, the teacher is available to work with students who need additional help. Slavin (1987b) reported that TAI "has had the largest achievement effects of all the cooperative learning methods" (p. 64).

Cooperative Integrated Reading and Composition (CIRC) is Slavin's (1987a) latest method, a comprehensive program for the teaching of language arts in the upper elementary grades. Students are assigned to teams composed of pairs from two different reading groups. The teachers work with one group, and the students in the other groups help each other by summarizing the stories, writing responses, practicing spelling or vocabulary, or editing papers. Rewards are given to teams rather than individuals, and scores are based on the average performance of all team members.

In addition to raising the achievement level of black students, cooperative learning methods have positive social outcomes as well. Race relations improve in desegregated schools where cooperative methods are employed (Schofield, 1982; Slavin & Madden, 1979). When students of different backgrounds must work together to accomplish a common goal and when the success of the group depends on the contribution of each individual member, students who otherwise do not interact begin to communicate and understand each other. (When the army desegregated in 1947, it discovered that white recruits abandoned their racist attitudes when their survival depended on cooperating with their new black peers.)

In summary, there are alternatives to tracking. Adler's Paideia Proposal, Oakes's curriculum organized around themes and ideas, and Slavin's cooperative instructional methods offer compelling options. What is certainly required if tracking and its inherent inequities are eliminated and teacher expectations are raised for black students is structural reorganization of schools and curriculum, as well as the rethinking of long-held assumptions about intelligence and ability.

RELEVANT FINDINGS FROM THE EFFECTIVE SCHOOLS RESEARCH

Researchers have recently begun to investigate and isolate school variables that positively relate to student achievement. This third school of thought, often called effective schools research, assumes that the differences in achievement among school-age children can be attributed to the variability in the schools (Edmonds, 1986). Edmonds and other investigators noticed that some schools that served low-income black students were characterized by low achievement and low expectations, indifferent, phlegmatic teachers and administrators, and unruly and apathetic students. On the other hand, there were schools that enrolled similar low-income students yet had quite different instructional climates. Students were learning; they were scoring at national norms on standardized tests. School buildings were orderly and pleasant, and parents and the community were proud of their schools.

These research findings called into question long-held views of prominent educators like Coleman (1966) and Jencks et al. (1972) that the child's home environment had a far greater impact on achievement than variables as such the quality of the school building, instructional materials and equipment, and the characteristics of the teachers and principals. Competent administrators and teachers of low-income black students do not outright dismiss Coleman's and Jenck's theses but accept the home factors as givens, usually out of the school's purview to directly influence or change. In these effective schools, the fact that a child is on welfare and perhaps living in a single-parent home is never used as an excuse to justify a student's nonachievement.

Ron Edmonds (1979) was one of the first researchers who attempted to identify the characteristics of effective schools for low-income black children. He found that effective schools had principals who were strong instructional leaders. They focused on the acquisition of skills in reading and mathematics. There was frequent and systematic monitoring of pupil progress in an orderly and safe school environment. Finally, the teachers in these schools had high expectations and believed that these students were capable of learning and that it was incumbent upon the school to teach them.

One of the most comprehensive reviews of the literature of factors associated with successful urban elementary schools was conducted by Clark, Lotto, and McCarthy (1980). They reviewed twelve hundred studies of urban schools and eliminated those that did not meet predetermined quality standards. In addition to the research studies, the team examined case studies, interviewed experts in the field, and observed exceptional urban elementary schools.

These researchers found the following six clusters of variables significant in influencing urban school-children's performance: leadership, teaching personnel, finances, resources and facilities, curriculum and instruction, and community resources.

The behavior of the designated leader, particularly the principal, significantly determined school success. Far more important than the leader's training, experience, and personal characteristics were the leader's attitude toward his/her school and expectations for success. These successful leaders were described by Clark, Lotto, and McCarthy (1980) as enablers, initiators, motivators, supporters, and goal setters.

The most significant teacher variable associated with school success was the quality of the staff development and in-service programs. The more specific and focused the training, the greater the effect. What is important about this finding is that teachers, with the guidance of effective principals, can be trained to modify their behavior and instructional strategies. The study also concluded that reduced teacher-student ratios are associated with school improvement. Although the literature is replete with contradictions to these generalizations, it appears that reduced class size produces limited results. However, in conjunction with an effective leader and other improvement factors, low teacher-student ratios are significant.

Successful schools in low-income communities have special project funds from federal, state, and local sources. Additional monies are required for urban school improvement. This observation by the researchers contradicts present federal (and some state) policies, which have significantly decreased funding for special projects in urban areas.

Instructional resources and facilities are weak predictors for successful schools. Clark, Lotto, and McCarthy (1980) state, "Resources and facilities are tools that can be strong or weak interventions, depending upon the principals and teachers who use them" (p. 469). This variable is, of course, related to the financial variable. Additional money for materials and equipment to be used by ineffective principals and teachers is a waste. Newly constructed buildings, instructional equipment, and supplies—computers, for example—do not make effective schools.

Effective urban schools have instructional programs that have clearly stated goals and objectives that are implemented and continually articulated by the principal to teachers, parents, and students. The learning environment is structured, and no single curricular organization or instructional strategy (except individualization) seems more effective than another. The particular strategy is less important than how the strategy meets the individual needs and learning style of the student.

Successful schools have parents who participate in school activities and have frequent contact with teachers and the principal. (This factor is discussed in detail later in this chapter.)

Hilliard (1988) warns that the effective school research, although important, focuses on the teaching and the assessment of minimum rather than maximum skills and that the professional effort to produce minimum competencies is different from that required to produce maximum competencies. This researcher suggests that some of the key variables for successful "maximum competencies" schools for black students include "high levels of academic preparation for the teaching staff; the development of a special ethos; a shared high-level academic mission among the faculty; and the extensive and appropriate use of well-conceived and well-planned field trips, outside speakers, and so forth" (p. 200). Levin's (1987) accelerated schools programs appear to embody many of these characteristics; however, more research and documentation of these schools are needed.

Glenn (1981), in a publication of the Center for Law and Education at Harvard, summarized the findings of effective schools research and concluded that effective schools have teachers and other adults who are committed to teaching poor and black children. There is a belief by these adults that black children can be taught to read, write, and compute. The curriculum is focused on reading, writing, and mathematics with systematic testing of students' mastery. Teachers have high expectations, and principals are strong leaders who maintain an orderly school environment. Parents are involved in their children's education.

The Instructional Leader

There is common agreement in the literature that effective schools have instructional leaders, usually principals, who exhibit traits and behaviors that are different from ineffective principals. Although leadership theory and research have long posited that there is no systematic relationship between personal traits and leadership (Jago, 1982; Owens, 1987), it now appears that "throwing out all the trait research and theories is less than wise" (Mazzarella, 1981, p. 17) and that constellations or clusters of traits rather than a single characteristic do correlate with leadership.

Of course, all effective principals are hardworking and dedicated; they want their students to learn. In effective schools that serve at-risk populations, these qualities alone are not sufficient. Effective principals of these types of schools have remarkable social and interpersonal skills that facilitate their working with a variety of people. They are more often extroverted than introverted, preferring face-to-face contact with students, teachers, and parents and verbal instead of written exchanges. Obviously, these principals are skilled communicators who vary their language and style of presentation to fit the audience and the situation. The audiences of these principals include such diverse groups as teachers, businesspeople, parents, policy-makers, and community and church members.

But excellent communication skills cannot exist without effective listening skills. These principals of low-income black schools listen unpatronizingly to parents, teachers, and students, act expeditiously on the issues of concern, and follow up, usually with a telephone call or brief note. Acting expeditiously should not be interpreted to mean that these principals respond in ways that always satisfy their various constituencies. They do not. Instead, they seek necessary information, use their professional experience and judgment, and make decisions that are defensible.

Like the teachers in the classroom, effective principals are energetic, active, and highly visible to students and teachers. They seem clear about goals and directions; they are secure enough about themselves and these goals that they are unthreatened by challenges or situations of high ambiguity and uncertainty, conditions that are prevalent in schools that serve black students. When well-conceived plans falter or unforeseen variables emerge, these principals enthusiastically rally their staff for renewed planning. They are attentive to the need to maintain and develop a strong school morale and healthy climate and often rely on their visionary leadership, optimism, and missionary zeal in unstable and uncertain circumstances.

This sense of clarity about who they are contributes to effective principals' proactive stance. Effective principals of at-risk schools often ignore imposed bureaucratic rules and regulations that are incompatible with their schools' needs and goals. They don't adhere to rigid chains of command or become incapacitated or frustrated by them. These effective principals move through—and often defy—bureaucratic mazes with the support of their teachers and the parents. Mazzarella (1981) stated, however, that these principals are not rebels or mavericks who are unaware or naive about power and survival. Quoting Blumberg and Greenfield, she noted:

> A characteristic of principals who lead seems to be that they behave in ways that enable them to be in charge of the job and not let the job be in charge of them. They are not pawns of the system. They seem to be adept at playing the games on which their survival depends, but they don't let the game playing consume too much of their energy (p. 33).

They are certainly change agents who are seldom overwhelmed or incapacitated by the conflicting demands of the job; they make new visions possible for their students and staff. Starratt described these principals: "They have a feel for the more dramatic possibilities inherent in most situations and are able to urge people to go beyond the routine, to break out of the mold into something lively and vibrant" (Sergiovanni et al., 1980, quoting Starratt, p. 18). Such school leaders inspire and motivate students, teachers, and parents.

Effective principals of black schools maintain a learning environment that is orderly and safe, yet never rigid and oppressive. Unfortunately, principals of these schools are often recruited to their positions because they can control crowds and discipline black students, particularly black males. For this reason, the ranks of secondary principals are over-represented by former male coaches, band directors, and veterans. No example is more glaring than the profile of Joe Clark, the much-publicized, highly commended law-and-order principal of Eastside High School of Patterson, New Jersey. Joe Clark believes "that if something is wrong, get tough about it—now" ("Getting Tough," 1988). He maintains discipline by carrying a bat and bullhorn and expelling unruly students and defiant teachers. This example of repressive, often violent, school leadership focuses primarily on intimidation and control over the physical movement of students, ignoring the role of the principal as the instructional leader of the school.

All of the previously stated positive traits and behaviors are important, but one of the most often ignored qualifications of a principal in a black at-risk school is that he or she must know how to observe classroom instruction and provide teachers with specific feedback about their strengths and weaknesses. Effective principals don't become distracted from attending to their number one priority—improving instruction that enhances student learning. They visit classrooms often and for extended periods of time. They feel comfortable in this role because they were master teachers themselves in similar settings. These principals often teach a class to reinforce their skills and to establish their credibility with their teachers. Because they know instruction, they are more skilled at recruiting competent teachers and dismissing incompetent ones. Their proficiency in manipulating bureaucracies facilitates this selection and dismissal process.

In summary, effective principals attend to school goals, ensure teacher competence, facilitate teaching and learning conditions, and motivate their teachers. They frequently articulate clear goals and criteria, emphasize collegiality, involve teachers in the decision-making process, recruit competent teachers, monitor teacher performance, provide staff development sessions that appeal to the needs of strong and weak teachers, manage learning time, maintain an orderly climate, facilitate teacher interaction, and involve the parents and the community (Hawley, et al., 1984c). The coordination and maintenance of these administrative tasks are difficult and require careful attention to the selection of principals and teachers. However, the evidence is that when effective principals are present in schools of perceived low achievers, students do learn.

PARENTAL INVOLVEMENT RESEARCH

One of the most difficult and unsolved problems of education is how to effectively involve black and low-income parents in the education of their children. Schools acknowledge the value of parental involvement, and the effective schools research has identified parental involvement as a critical factor (Edmonds, 1979). However, there are too few inner-city, predominantly black schools that have programs designed to promote meaningful participation by parents. (See *Journal of Negro Education*, Summer 1988, volume 57, number 3 for descriptions of model programs.)

This lack of participation is not related to lack of interest by black parents. Historically, slaves used education as the primary strategy for liberation. Because whites passed laws in some states forbidding the education of slaves, blacks risked their lives in order to learn how to read and write. This strong historical tradition and cultural value still exists in the black community. Although some ethnic minorities have made significant gains through political and economic strategies (Greer, 1972), the primary vehicle to middle-class status for black people is still through education and training. In the past, blacks and other minorities succeeded in school because their parents valued and strongly supported education (Berube, 1983; Sowell, 1976).

All parents value education for their children, but black parents' aspirations have been described as culture-specific, compelling, and passionate (Lightfoot, 1981; Peters, 1981). Black parents understand that the only way out of poverty is through education, and consequently they have more emotional involvement in their schools because schools have been concrete representations of black people's hopes and dreams. Honig (1987) stated that black parents overwhelmingly support high standards, tough courses, and more homework for their children and that they "realize that the ability to compete, both in school and in the job market, is their children's greatest chance for achieving lifelong success" (p. 12). As technology rapidly increases the complexity of work, and the demand for unskilled and semiskilled labor disappears, black parents' aspirations for their children and expectations for schools can be expected to rise.

Such high and unrealistic expectations for schooling can only result in unfulfilled desires and disappointments. Black parents often react with hostility or withdraw physically and emotionally when their children fail to succeed, fearing that their offspring may never escape poverty. Like majority parents, they feel a sense of responsibility for their children's school failure; negative messages from schools serve only as additional obstructions and barriers.

Why have schools not capitalized on this cultural value? Lightfoot (1978) has provided insight into the problem. She stated, "The dissonance between black parents and teachers, therefore, does not lie in the conflicting values attached to education, but in the misperceptions they have of each other" (p. 160). The lack of cultural synchronization between the black family and the schools, discussed in Chapter 2, is a primary factor that explains black parents' nonparticipation. Schools often treat black parents as nuisances to be tolerated or, worse, as causes for their children's failure. Teachers often believe that low-income black parents are confrontive, hostile, ignorant, and incompetent. When teachers have direct contact with parents, they prefer black parents who are "obsequious, appreciative, and uncritical" (Lightfoot, 1978, p. 37). Some black parents understand this attitude, and many refrain from directly confronting insensitive school personnel for fear of retribution. These parents believe that teachers and principals will punish their children because the parents have criticized or questioned teachers.

Because some black parents speak nonstandard English and do not attend Parent-Teacher Association (PTA) meetings, write notes to teachers, volunteer as helpers, or request conferences, school personnel assume lack of interest or negligence. These negative beliefs about black parents are not specific to low-income black parents but pertain to middle-class black parents as well. Smith and Andrew's (1988) study of an affluent school district in northern Virginia found that teachers believed that the black children lived in culturally deprived homes with apathetic single parents on welfare, although the actual data dramatically contradicted this profile. The teachers assumed that all the black children came from low-income families with uninterested parents, and the teachers tended to treat students and parents in stereotypical ways. It appears that the barriers that interfere with black parents' participation in school are based not entirely on class distinctions, but on generalized attitudes and perceptions that the black family is culturally deficient and the home environment antithetical to school achievement.

The desegregation of schools has also exacerbated the problems. Black students have disproportionately carried the weight of desegregating the nation's schools. Bused out of their neighborhoods into predominantly white communities, students and their parents often feel alienated and excluded from the schools. Black parents find it difficult to attend meetings, volunteer, and communicate with teachers when their children are bused out of their neighborhoods. These black parents have few opportunities to see their children's teachers during school hours. The physical distance directly contributes to the inevitable psychological distance.

Desegregation has also contributed to dwindling numbers of black teachers in schools that black students attend. (See Chapter 2 for a more detailed discussion.) Prior to desegregation, black parents communicated with school officials in the black neighborhoods where they both lived. Black churches, lodges, barber and beauty shops, and benevolent societies were places where parents and teachers informally and frequently exchanged and shared information about black children. Desegregation eliminated these informal communication structures because both the black and the white teachers of black children no longer lived in the black communities.

Because black children are twice as likely as white children to be born to an uneducated teenaged mother and three times as likely to live in a female-headed household (Edelman, 1986), their mothers often find it difficult to converse with school personnel. When they do attend school functions, effective communication seldom takes place because teachers have no training in effective parent-teacher relationships with uneducated mothers and/or adolescent mothers.

In secondary schools, the barriers to parental participation are more obstinate (Tangri & Moles, 1987). Adolescents discourage their parents from being too visible at school because the students' friends often react negatively. Slaughter (1986) discovered that the black students whose parents were actively involved in school activities were least likely to be chosen as a preferred peer. These children were not popular because their peer culture ostracized students whose parents participated in school activities. Consequently, messages, announcements, newsletters, and report cards often fail to reach parents. Parents of high school students do not question their children as frequently about their course work because the content is more difficult to understand. Drilling and practicing the multiplication tables are considerably more manageable to low-income and working-class parents than providing assistance with geometry. Another barrier is that the number of school personnel a parent must communicate with dramatically increases at the middle and high school levels. The typical high school student, for instance, has seven teachers, a counselor, several assistant principals, and a principal. Establishing an effective communications network with each of these school functionaries is a logistical and psychological nightmare.

The Relationship Between Parental Involvement and Student Achievement

Former Secretary of Education Bennett (1986) is a strong advocate of parental involvement. He stated: "Parents belong at the center of a young child's education. The single best way to improve elementary education is to strengthen parents' role in it" (p. 126). There is much evidence to support Bennett's statement; the research data suggest that parents' involvement in their children's education improves their children's academic achievement. (For literature reviews, see Becher, 1984; Gordon and Breivogel, 1976; Henderson, 1987; Seginer, 1983). One obvious weakness of most of these reviewed studies is that they have primarily focused on middle-class white families and ignored the role of low-income or minority families.

One study (Brantlinger, 1985) interviewed low-income parents about their perceptions of favoritism in their children's schools. These parents felt that schools favored academically advanced, wealthy, and university-affiliated people in academic as well as nonacademic areas. Previous studies have confirmed low-income people's feeling of alienation, power-lessness, low sense of control, and cultural estrangement in schools (Seeman, 1975; White, 1980). However, the literature that has focused on black or low-income parents (Benson et al., 1980; Clark, 1983; Comer, 1986; Hoover-Dempsey et al., 1987; Lightfoot, 1978; Revicki, 1981) has concluded that there are positive benefits derived from parental participation, primarily the improved academic achievement of their children. The implications of this often-cited conclusion must be scrutinized carefully. What is parental involvement? Are all parental educational activities equally beneficial to students? Is the relationship between parental involvement and academic achievement spurious? Do parents who participate in their children's education enhance their performance, or are the parents of high-achieving students more inclined to participate in school activities?

Defining Parental Involvement

Slaughter (1986) has made a distinction between the terms *parental participation* and *parental involvement*. She defined participation as direct engagement in school activities and involvement as the support of the child's schooling. Most schools value both of these activities but focus only on the participation dimension. Schools measure the success of parent participation by counting the numbers of parents that attend ritualistic events like parent conferences, PTA meetings, open houses, fund-raisers, sports events, and musical and dramatic festivals. If there is some type of communication during these "contrived occasions" (Lightfoot, 1978, p. 28), it is usually one-way—teachers and other school officials telling parents about their children's progress or students performing to audiences of admiring parents.

Besides the role of parents as audience, Swap (1987) identified other options: parents as helpers (chaperons, fund-raisers, and school volunteers); parents as experts (computer lab assistants and speakers); parents as decision makers in governance (advisory board members and task force members); and parents as teachers in the home. Are all these parental roles equally beneficial to students? The literature reviews of Hawley et al. (1984b) and Tangri and Moles (1987) suggest not only that these options for school participation are of unequal importance but that parents are not equally interested in serving in all of these roles.

During the Great Society programs of the 1960s, black parents' participation in governance was mandated for programs like Head Start, Follow Through, Chapter One, and Parent Child Care Centers. Although there are testimonials praising such efforts, there is little empirical evidence that parents are interested in governance or policymaking, nor is there evidence that parental participation in such matters is related to student achievement (Hawley et al., 1984b; Tangri & Moles, 1987). Perhaps parents' apathy regarding these governance matters is related to parents' perceptions that they have only marginal roles in decision making and that their participation has little to do with the achievement of their children.

What appears to be a crucial role for black parents is their role as teachers in the home. It is the role that parents prefer and the one directly related to the achievement of their children. Ianni (1987) and Walberg (1984) stated that parents, regardless of their socioeconomic status, significantly increase their children's academic learning when they perform the role of home instructor. As supervisors of the home curriculum, these parents talk to their children every day about lessons learned, graded papers, and assignments due. They read to their children, take them to the library, supervise and check homework, encourage them, and closely monitor television watching.

The most detailed description of the way black parents participate in the curriculum of the home is provided by Clark (1983) in the book *Family Life and School Achievement: Why Poor Black Children Succeed or Fail.* Clark's study was conducted with ten poor black families in Chicago; half of the families had high-achieving children, and half had low achievers. There were one- and two-parent families in both groups. For six months, Clark interviewed and observed the families, students, and teachers. What he discovered was that the difference between high- and low-achieving poor black students was parenting styles. He distinguished between two styles: sponsored versus unsponsored independence. The black parents of the high achievers exhibited sponsored independence parenting styles. They talked to their children often; visited their children's school frequently; assisted, coached, and instructed; established clear and consistent rules regarding behavior; and had high expectations for present school success and future college attendance.

The low achievers' parents, on the other hand, displayed unsponsored independence. They had low expectations for their children; seldom went to their children's school; did not expect them to attend college; did not encourage, assist, or support; did not define rules of conduct or the boundaries of parent and child roles; and failed to monitor the way their children spent their time. Clark's findings are supported by the works of Durkin (1984) and Lee (1984).

Ways Schools Can Assist Black Parents

These findings suggest that schools must assist other agencies in providing low-income black parents with training that focuses on strategies to help their children achieve in school. Schools can schedule such training as sessions of the PTA or a special evening meeting. They can also seek special funding for a comprehensive program of parent training. These activities should be planned and executed with the assistance of black churches, social service agencies, and volunteer service organizations in the community. The three areas that warrant skills development are (1) general parenting skills, (2) teaching, and (3) advocating.

Parenting (Clark, 1983). Black parents should set clear, consistent, and fair rules regarding appropriate and acceptable behavior both in the home and at school. Because the school, home, church, and playgrounds demand different sets of behaviors, parents must help their children understand the contingencies of these varied situations. In order to reinforce these behaviors, children should be praised when they perform well in school and in the home, and criticisms of poor performance and rule violations should be eliminated.

Parents need to demonstrate the behaviors they want their child to model such as reading books and newspapers and frequenting the library, museums, zoos, and theaters. If a parent has difficulty reading, then the parent should enroll in an adult literacy program.

Independence and problem solving are nurtured in homes where children participate in decision making. For instance, children can decide the clothing they wear to school or their lunch menu. Family meetings are important opportunities for group decision making as well as occasions to discuss openly and clarify positions regarding premarital sex and drug and alcohol abuse. Family disagreements and confrontations are best handled in a family meeting format instead of in reactive responses to misbehavior like corporal punishment. It is helpful to identify and maintain contact with families or individuals in the community who have similar educational and moral values. These persons are potential support systems that can be called upon, particularly if the family is in crisis.

Teaching (Edwards, 1987). If trained, black parents, especially of elementary children, can be effective teachers in the home. For example, parents can learn to provide a quiet place, even a small space, for their child to do homework with a mutually agreed upon time schedule. Parents can be trained to ask questions that keep them informed of their child's progress. For example, every day parents should ask specific questions about their children's school day, such as, How was school today? What did you do in math? science, etc? Where are your graded tests or homework papers? Did you have a quiz today? What grade do you think you made? Children should be asked if they know the correct answer to incorrect responses on graded papers. Ask: What questions did you answer today? Did you get punished today? Why?

Unfortunately, parents provide learning activities at home that are replications of school activities. Basic skills can be taught by using everyday home activities—measuring ingredients while cooking, making change for bus rides, spelling and identifying the names of common household items, adding the cost of grocery items, classifying similar and dissimilar articles, and listening to records and copying the lyrics on paper. The point is to design learning activities in which the child is not likely to participate in school, such as composing a play, song, or poem for performance at some special family event or after dinner on Sunday. Finally, parents have a responsibility to limit the number of hours their children watch television. Black children watch significantly more television than do white children, a factor possibly related to their lack of school achievement.

Advocating (National Committee for Citizens in Education, 1985; Rotter, Robinson, & Fey, 1987). Black students' school failure is related to the absence of strong advocates. Parents are the most effective advocates for their children, but low-income minority parents lack the necessary skills to perform this role. Black parents need guidance from community agencies and churches about how to be effective advocates within the school setting.

Black parents should visit the school principal and ask for data concerning the school's achievement scores on standardized measures. How does this school compare to others in the district? Is there a plan or strategy to increase the scores? How many teachers in the school have advanced degrees? How many hold permanent teaching certificates? How many of the teachers have been at this school for five years or more? How many teachers have five or more years of teaching experience? How often are teachers, administrators, and staff evaluated? Is discipline a problem in this school? How many students were expelled or suspended during the last school year? What proactive measures are being implemented to decrease the number of expulsions and suspensions? How are students placed in the various ability groups? How can students be moved from one level to another after the initial placement has been made? Can parents observe their child's class? Can parents review their child's permanent record? Are parents routinely notified when their child has a behavioral or academic problem?

One of the most valuable tools is the parent-teacher conference. Single parents should consider bringing another interested adult like a grandmother or uncle, someone who provides more than a one-person support system for the child. Information about the student and the family should be shared with the teacher if it helps the teacher to understand and teach the child better. Black parents are often reluctant to share information with their child's teacher about family circumstances (Wyche & Wyche, 1984), such as illness, death, divorce, or separation. They fear, often justifiably, that teachers might use personal family data to confirm negative expectations and stereotypes.

Parents must be active participants, not merely listeners, in these meetings with teachers. There are several questions that parents should ask: What is your impression of my son/daughter? What are her strengths and weaknesses? Does she raise her hand often to answer questions? Is homework turned in on time? What grades and papers do you have to share with me? Is he performing at grade level? What do these standardized scores mean? Does he misbehave in class? Has my child been absent from school this year? What days? Where does my child sit in this class? Does he get along with his classmates? Does he participate in group activities? Does she work independently? Is she alert and enthusiastic about learning? With whom does she play or talk most often? Do you have a plan to increase my child's performance? How can I help? Parent-teacher conferences are more productive when parents are punctual and positive, bring written questions, take notes, and follow up immediately by scheduling a subsequent meeting.

Finally, black parents should attend PTA and local board meetings and raise issues of concern. If there is a need for organized educational support groups, such as homework assistance centers or homework hotlines, then these meetings are an appropriate forum for discussion.

In summary, strategies for improving the school achievement of black students should involve interventions directed at (1) decreasing the cultural discontinuity by attending to students' learning styles, their values, language, and history, as well as the many resources in the home and the community; (2) increasing teacher expectations by effective instruction in schools administered by effective school leaders and eliminating rigid and inflexible ability groups and tracks; and (3) helping parents and relatives to assist and reinforce school learning.

6

Implications for Training and Staff Development

This chapter outlines some generic competencies that can serve as guidelines for in-service staff development programs as well as preservice teacher education programs. More effort must be spent in training current black and white preservice as well as in-service teachers to instruct minority and high-risk students effectively. This emphasis on training gives recognition to the fact that both black and white teachers tend to teach best those who need their assistance the least—middle-class students. What is needed is the development of preservice and in-service programs to train teachers and administrators of at-risk black students who are presently perceived as "special," but who will be by the next decade the majority of public school children.

Given that the majority of teachers are presently and will continue to be white, middle-class females, can this population be trained to be effective teachers of black children? Can part of the problem become part of the solution? The answer to both questions is yes. Two primary factors contribute to the unequal treatment of black students in school: prejudicial attitudes and lack of appropriate training. Prejudice, the affective factor, is a learned response to socialization and enculturalization. Lack of knowledge and skills, the cognitive and behavioral factors, are learning deficiencies. Neither is a genetic predisposition; they are both alterable and modifiable through in-service staff development and preservice teacher education programs.

Guskey's (1986) model is the recommended staff development strategy. He proposed, contrary to popular approaches, that the best way to change teachers' attitudes is first to provide them with staff development training that will improve pupils' learning, motivation, attendance, and attitudes. Guskey stated:

Clearly, teachers are attracted to staff development programs because they believe these activities can potentially expand their knowledge and skills, contribute to their growth, and enhance their effectiveness with students. But it is also clear that teachers carry with them to staff development programs a very pragmatic orientation. What they hope to gain through staff development programs are specific, concrete, and practical ideas that directly relate to the day-to-day operation of their classrooms (p. 6).

For schools that enroll black students, this research implies that teachers are more likely to address their lack of cultural synchronization and prejudicial beliefs and attitudes after they have received training that has improved their instructional practices and has produced positive changes in student learning outcomes.

PRECONDITIONS FOR EFFECTIVE STAFF DEVELOPMENT

In order for any staff development program to "make a difference," the following conditions should be attended to:

1. The staff development program should adopt the Guskey Model of Teacher Change. That is, it should first focus on the improvement of teachers' classroom practices before attempting to change attitudes and beliefs.

2. The staff development program should be a whole school approach involving teachers, administrators, and staff persons.

3. Each adult in the school should desire to continue to work with black and at-risk students and have a willingness to grow personally and professionally. Staff who prefer working in other school settings should be assisted in finding a more suitable placement.

4. The staff development program should be conceptualized as a long-range project requiring at least two sessions a month over the school year. This condition necessitates a commitment of time and money.

5. Planning and decision making should be collaborative and participatory.

6. It should be acknowledged that the benefits of training will require time and that change will be gradual.

7. Principals and other school administrators should follow up with visits to teachers' classrooms, individual conferences with teachers, and specific feedback.

8. As teachers prefer to help each other, release time should be arranged for teachers to visit and confer with each other.

9. Parents, students, and community leaders should serve in an advisory capacity to the staff development program.

The focus of the training should be directed at eliminating prejudicial attitudes and sources of hidden conflict; training teachers in effective instruction; managing the classroom and developing disciplinary strategies; concurrently training principals in effective leadership skills; developing school policies that undergird the achievement of black students; and, finally, developing programs to enhance parental involvement.

STAFF DEVELOPMENT COMPETENCIES FOR POLICY DEVELOPMENT

Attention must be given to the policies related to curriculum, students, staff, and organizational development.

1. The curriculum should include the study of the history and culture of Afro-Americans.

2. The curriculum should include opportunities for critical discussion of racism, sexism, and classism.

3. The curriculum should be multicultural.

4. The curriculum should not be tracked with rigid homogeneous ability groupings that foster race and class stereotypes.

5. The school environment should be orderly, pleasant, and safe, not autocratic and overly restrictive.

6. Testing procedures and assessment should emphasize diagnosis rather than the labeling or categorizing of students.

7. Disciplinary procedures and policies should be formulated by teachers, parents, and students and dispensed fairly and consistently.

8. There should be a system for rewarding and recognizing excellent performances by students, teachers, and staff.

9. There should always be sufficient resources available for equipment, supplies, repairs, and maintenance of facilities.

10. Teachers should feel secure in their job, about their personal belongings, and about their personal safety.
11. Mechanisms and structures should be designed so teachers can develop a sense of cohesiveness and collegiality.

STAFF DEVELOPMENT COMPETENCIES FOR PREJUDICE REDUCTION

Principals and teachers should have an understanding and sensitivity about

1. the nature of racism and prejudice from a cognitive as well as affective perspective
2. Afro-Americans' and other minorities' cultural heritage and history (Bennett, 1969)
3. the unique characteristics of black children's relational style of processing information (Hale-Benson 1986; Shade, 1982)
4. black children's language and the instructional methods necessary for translating this language to standard English
5. skills and behaviors brought to school by black children that have made them more developmentally precocious infants than are majority children (Freedman, 1974)
6. the differences in black and white parenting styles (McAdoo, 1981; Spencer, 1983)
7. the role black parents and their community play in students' achievement (Billingsley, 1968)
8. the negative impact of low expectations and the resultant self-fulfilling prophecy (Baron, Tom, & Cooper, 1985)

STAFF DEVELOPMENT COMPETENCIES FOR TEACHERS

Teachers should be competent in their subject matter as well as fluent in verbal and written communication. In addition, they should employ instructional strategies that seem to be associated with effective instruction for minority high-risk students (Brophy, 1982; Brown, Palincsar, & Purcell, 1986; Levine, Levine, & Eubanks, 1985; Ramírez & Castañeda, 1974).

These teachers should be aware that:

1. all students are capable of learning and that student failure is a challenge for the teacher.

2. effective teachers provide their students with opportunities to learn and practice.

3. effective teachers have well-orchestrated, well-managed class-rooms in which transitions are quick and efficient with minimal disruptions. Students seem to know what to do and when to do it.

4. there is a match between the difficulty level of the material and the students' ability to master the materials successfully.

5. effective teachers teach—demonstrating, modeling, explaining, writing, giving feedback, reviewing.

6. supportive learning environments with caring and sensitive teachers are essential.

7. successful teachers of minority students emphasize higher-order skills, avoiding a heavy reliance on rote learning and drill and practice.

8. effective teachers of minority students assess cognitive styles and know how to teach bicognitively, using field-sensitive and field-independent teaching behaviors, instructional styles, and class-room environments.

9. effective teachers frequently depart from "teacher-proof" curriculum guides and directives.

10. effective teachers of black children often use collaborative and cooperative instructional methods.

11. effective teachers of minority students often develop idiosyncratic styles of teaching and relating to their students.

STAFF DEVELOPMENT COMPETENCIES FOR PRINCIPALS

Principals should understand the findings of the effective schools research (Brookover, 1985; Clark, Lotto, & McCarthy, 1980; Edmonds, 1979; Sizemore, 1985), including the following precepts:

1. Effective principals believe that black children can learn if taught.

2. Effective principals recognize and reward teachers.

3. Effective principals establish procedures to monitor students' progress.

4. Effective principals often take risks and disagree with their superiors.

5. Effective principals know instruction and supervise and coach their teachers by visiting classrooms every day.

6. Effective principals encourage and train parents to be partners in the child's education.

7. Effective principals have goals and well-conceived plans to achieve them.

8. Effective principals recruit competent teachers and involve them in decision making and planning; they also dismiss incompetent ones.

9. Effective principals provide meaningful staff development sessions for their staff.

10. Effective principals have personal and professional respect for their teachers and staff, often protecting them from unwarranted demands by central office personnel, parents, and students.

11. Effective principals eliminate barriers to effective teaching, such as heavy paperwork responsibilities, unnecessary committee work, and lack of materials and supplies.

STAFF DEVELOPMENT COMPETENCIES FOR PARENT EDUCATION

Principals and teachers must also be trained to communicate effectively with black parents. Educators presently receive minimal training in techniques to enhance home-school relationships, particularly in low-income or black homes. Because each community has particular needs and a unique relationship with the school, care must be taken to design a parental involvement program that includes input from a variety of parents, teachers, and community leaders.

However, there are certain minimum competencies that seem applicable to all parental involvement programs for black parents (Rich, 1987; Rotter, Robinson, & Fey, 1987; Swap, 1987).

School administrators should:

1. prepare a clearly written handbook for parents and students outlining expectations for conduct regarding behavior in classes, dress, drug and alcohol use, thefts, assaults, truancy, homework, testing, grading, and report cards.

2. prepare a practical, jargon-free, usable handout for parents explaining curriculum objectives and standardized test score interpretations (Dyer, 1980).

3. communicate with parents in a variety of forms—PTAs, conferences, newsletters, school calendars, open houses, course syllabi, grade reports. For conferences and PTA meetings, provide child care through student organizations.

4. report absences to parents. The use of computerized telephone dialing systems has proved effective in many urban systems.

5. train secretarial and custodial staffs to be pleasant and helpful to parents who visit the school or call.

6. provide in-service training to teachers regarding ways to assist parents in helping their children at home. Train them also in effective conferencing skills such as attending conferences, listening, paraphrasing, and responding.

7. establish an open-door policy for parents.

8. because the population of schools that serve black children is often very transient, provide ongoing orientation sessions for new parents in the school.

9. establish a "homework hotline" for students and their parents who need assistance with assignments. Consider supervised homework study sessions before school, during lunch, and after school.

10. provide release time for teachers who meet with parents during evening hours or make home visits.

11. establish a lending library of educational games and supplementary instruction materials for parents. Provide training sessions on how to use them.

12. when black students are bused outside of their communities, conduct meetings in libraries, community centers, or churches in the black community.

13. maintain an orderly, clean, safe, and physically attractive physical plant. Parents particularly notice these conditions.

14. invite community groups to use the school for community meet-
    ings and evening classes and to use the gym and the track for
    physical fitness.
15. provide parents with information about adult education programs
    and social service agencies in their community.

When communicating with black parents, teachers should

1. avoid educational jargon and communicate in a language that is
   understood and in a style that is inviting and warm.
2. avoid sitting behind a desk or barrier. Provide adult chairs for
   parents so that teachers are not peering down at parents.
3. describe the student's classroom conduct in specific, behavioral
   terms. Avoid terms such as "enthusiastic, uninterested, bad attitude." Describe the behavior that led to the conclusion that the
   student was, for instance, uninterested in school.
4. allow enough time for parents to discuss concerns. A minimum
   of thirty minutes is a good rule of thumb.
5. prepare for the conference by compiling samples of the child's
   work and standardized test scores. Teachers should let the parents
   know that they understand the child by discussing the child's
   emotional, social, and physical progress, as well as academic
   progress. Include a personal anecdote such as an interesting or
   funny story the child told in class.
6. send notes home or call parents when problems first surface. If
   parent does not respond, then visit the home.
7. leave each session with a parent on a positive note. Do not be defensive
   or assign blame for the child's academic or behavioral problem.
8. grade and comment on all homework and class assignments. Ask
   the students to have their parents sign all papers to ensure that
   they are informed and to enhance your credibility.
9. invite parents and grandparents to visit your classroom.

The identification of effective strategies to raise the achievement of
black students is a first step in addressing the problem. Teachers, principals, and parents of black children need to develop these competencies
as equal partners in a collaborative and cooperative venture, working to
adapt these recommendations to local interests and needs. Effective
schools have their own distinct culture, processes, and structures that

evolve in concert with the requirements of the community, the instructional needs of the students, the professional needs of the staff, the history of the school, and community politics (Irvine, 1988c). In this sense, no two schools are ever alike. However, the summary of the literature presented in this chapter does support the argument that we have enough empirical evidence to design, implement, and administer effective schools for all students, regardless of race and social class.

The outlined preconditions and competencies can serve as a framework for in-service as well as preservice training. The key to retaining the many teachers who are now leaving the profession, particularly in schools that serve at-risk black students, is to provide them with psychological, emotional, and instructional support and systematic in-service training. This training is obviously lacking in most preservice programs, and only recently have teacher education institutions begun to discuss the need to broaden their curriculum to include a multicultural perspective. However, much remains to be done.

7

Conclusion: Changing Schools for Future Challenges

This book describes significant factors associated with the failure of black students in school. The dissonance between the prescriptive ideologies and the descriptive practices was examined with particular attention to the negative effects of the hidden curriculum, tracking, and discriminatory disciplinary practices. The interpersonal context between students and teachers was described as a lack of cultural synchronization, a situation in which teachers do not share a common understanding of verbal and nonverbal language, manner of personal presentation, and ways of processing information and knowledge. The decreasing numbers of minority teachers have contributed to this problem. Lack of cultural responsiveness results in negative expectations by teachers and by the students themselves and in a pattern of differential teacher-student interactions in the classroom. The obvious outcome for black students is school failure. The final chapters were devoted to strategies and competencies for training teachers, administrators, and parents.

In summary, there are no quick and simple solutions, no single program or packaged interventions, no one way to teach black children. The foundation for success and a prerequisite for black student achievement appear to be committed, caring, dedicated, well-trained teachers who are not afraid, resentful, or hostile and who genuinely want to teach at these schools. This supportive relationship between teacher and student is a fundamental necessity from which all other solutions and interventions emerge. These teachers are "warm demanders" (Vasquez, 1988) who serve as role models, motivators, facilitators, guides, coaches, and mediators of learning for black students.

Teachers of low-income black students must serve another crucial function, as cultural translators. This statement implies that teachers should become bicultural—thoroughly knowledgeable and sensitive about black children's language, style of presentation, community values, traditions, legends, myths, history, symbols, and norms. They must serve as conduits through which culturally encapsulated, monocultural minority youngsters learn dual repertoires of behaviors and "cognitive switching" (Ramírez & Castañeda, 1974) in order that the children can function effectively in the culture of the school and the culture of the community. This new role does not imply that the culture of black and minority students is inferior, but it reflects the impertinence and obstinacy of schools in accommodating the culture of minority students.

Where did poor, successful black children learn the majority culture in decades past? Why should teachers perform this difficult job now? Before desegregation, the black community included poor, working-class, and middle-class people, and black teachers and other professionals were cultural translators. It was not uncommon to find black teachers and black maids attending the same church and living in the same neighborhood. This diverse community was stabilized by and revolved around common middle-class values and aspirations. Today, many impoverished black students are isolated in neighborhoods where they seldom see, not to mention know, people who work, speak standard English, or live in two-parent families. The radical transformation from heterogeneity to homogeneity has left some poor black communities isolated and often forgotten. There are no cultural translators, and educators must accept the challenges of these new responsibilities.

These challenges must be accepted because schools are dramatically changing. As the twenty-first century rapidly approaches, education is facing a serious dilemma. The "typical" student that pedagogy and educational prescriptions are designed for is an endangered species. Highly motivated, achievement-oriented, white middle-class students from two-parent families are becoming scarce in most school systems—rural, suburban, and urban. In ten years, these students will be even more rare. Hodgkinson's (1988) and Coates and Jarratt's (1987) data confirm that divorce, delayed marriage, delayed childbirth, declining fertility rates among white middle-class women, increasing fertility among poor minority women, and the influx of immigrants from Mexico, Asia, and the Caribbean will completely alter the way educators will administer schools and instruct students. Unless the education profession makes reforms to accommodate these students, then the year 2000 will not bode well for education and society at large. There will be a large pool of middle-class, white aged who will be asked to support financially the poor, nonwhite public-school children who are being taught by middle-class, white female teachers trained in the pedagogy of the 1960s and who work in schools with administrative structures and hierarchies designed for schools in the 1900s.

Schools must be redesigned to accommodate the needs of these students, and these decisions must be made at the school-site level. Some schools have experimented with school-based management, community-based boards of education, schools within a school, multiple-age grade levels, and homogeneous ability grouping. In addition, teachers must be rewarded for their efforts, given autonomy and flexibility to teach, and treated like professionals. When teachers feel alienated and helpless to influence school policy, they "tend to disparage students, consider them unteachable, hold them personally responsible for failure, and consider themselves powerless to effect change institutionally or individually" (Fine, 1988, p. 111).

These factors, often ignored, will contribute to the growing numbers of black children at risk—children who will not have the necessary skills to find jobs and become economically independent adults. The Committee for Economic Development (cited in W. T. Grant Commission, 1988) estimated that each class of school failures and dropouts costs the nation $240 billion in lost earnings and foregone taxes. Billions more are spent on these dropouts for crime control, welfare, and health and social services. It seems clear that the only viable alternative is to educate these children effectively not only because it is the fair and just thing to do but because we cannot afford not to.

References

Aaron, R., and Powell, G. 1982. Feedback practices as a function of teacher and pupil race during reading groups instruction. *Journal of Negro Education* 51:50–59.

Adair, A.V. 1984. *Desegregation: The illusion of black progress*. Lanham, Md. : University Press of America.

Adler, M. 1982. *The Paideia Proposal*. New York: Macmillan.

Allen, W.R. 1984, April. *Research on black students in higher education: Trends, issues, and prospects*. Paper presented at the meeting of the American Educational Research Association, New Orleans, La.

Allington, R.L. 1983. The reading instruction provided readers of different reading abilities. *The Elementary School Journal* 83:549–59.

Aloia, G.; Maxwell, J.; and Aloia, S. 1981. Influence of a child's race and the EMR label on initial impressions of regular classroom teachers. *American Journal of Mental Deficiency* 85:619–23.

Anderson, J.A. 1988. Cognitive styles and multicultural populations. *Journal of Teacher Education* 39:2–9.

Anderson, J.G. 1975. The consequences of bureaucratic structure. In *Theoretical dimensions of educational administration*, edited by W.G. Monahan, 264–77. New York: Macmillan.

Anrig, G.R. 1986. Teacher education and teacher training: The rush to mandate. *Phi Delta Kappan* 67:447–51.

Anyon, J. 1981. Social class and the hidden curriculum of work. In *Curriculum and instruction*, edited by H.A. Giroux, A.N. Penna, and W.F. Pinar, 317–41. Berkeley: McCutchan Publishing.

_____. 1983. Social class and the hidden curriculum of work. In *The hidden curriculum and moral education*, edited by H. Giroux and D. Purpel, 143–67. Berkeley: McCutchan Publishing.

Apple, M., and King, N. 1983. What do schools teach? In *The hidden curriculum and moral education*, edited by H. Giroux and D. Purpel, 82–99. Berkeley: McCutchan Publishing.

Asante, M.K. 1988. *Afrocentricity*. Trenton, N.J. : Africa World Press, Inc.

Au, K.H. 1980. Participation structures in a reading lesson with Hawaiian children: Analysis of a culturally appropriate instructional event. *Anthropology of Education Quarterly* 11:91–115.

Baker, S.H. 1973. Teacher effectiveness and social class as factors in teacher expectancy effects on pupils' scholastic achievement. (Doctoral dissertation, Clark University.) *Dissertation Abstracts International* 34:2376A.

Banks, J.A. 1988. Ethnicity, class, cognitive, and motivational styles: Research and teaching implications. *Journal of Negro Education* 57:452–66.

Baratz, J., and Baratz, S. 1972. Black culture on black terms: A rejection of the social pathology model. In *Rappin' and stylin' out*, edited by T. Kochman, 3–16. Urbana, Ill. : University of Illinois Press.

Baratz, J.C. 1986. *Black participation in the teacher pool*. New York: Carnegie Corporation.

Barnes, W.J. 1978. Student-teacher dyadic interaction in desegregated high school classrooms. *Western Journal of Black Studies* 2:132–37.

Baron, D.E. 1975. Nonstandard English, composition, and the academic establishment. *College English* 37:176–83.

Baron, R.M.; Tom, D.Y.; and Cooper, H.M. 1985. Social class, race and teacher expectations. In *Teacher expectancies*, edited by J.B. Dusek, 251–69. Hillsdale, N.J. : Lawrence Erlbaum Associates.

Beady, C.H., and Hansell, S. 1981. Teacher race and expectations for student achievement. *American Education Research Journal* 18:191–206.

Becher, R.M. 1984. *Parent involvement: A review of research and principles of successful practice*. Washington, D.C. : National Institute of Education. (ERIC Document Reproduction Service No. ED 247 032.)

Becker, H.J. 1986. *Instructional uses of school computers*. Baltimore, Md. : Johns Hopkins University.

Bennett, C. 1980. Student initiated interaction as an indicator of interracial acceptance. *Journal of Classroom Interaction* 15:1–10.

Bennett, C.I. 1986. *Comprehensive multicultural education*. Boston: Allyn and Bacon.

Bennett, L. 1969. *Before the Mayflower: A history of black America*. Chicago: Johnson Publishing.

Bennett, W.J. 1986. First lessons. *Phi Delta Kappan* 68:125–28.

Benson, C.S.; Medrich, E.A.; and Buckley, S. 1980. A new view of school efficiency: Household time contributions to school achievement. In *School finance policies and practices. The 1980's: A decade of conflict*, edited by J. Guthrie, 169–204. Cambridge, Mass. : Ballinger.

Berliner, D.C. 1984. The half-full glass: A review of research on teaching. In *Using what we know about teaching*, edited by P.L. Hosford, 51–77. Alexandria, Va.: Association for Supervision and Curriculum Development.

Berube, M.R. 1983. Educating the urban poor. *The Urban Review* 15:151–63.

Beyer, B.K. 1987. *Practical strategies for teaching of thinking*. Boston: Allyn and Bacon.

Billingsley, A. 1968. *Black families in white America*. Englewood Cliffs, N.J. : Prentice Hall.

Blacks sliding backwards as college-bound rate declines. 1985, June 19. *Report on Educational Research* 17:7.

Bloom, B.S. 1976. *Human characteristics and school learning*. New York: McGraw-Hill.

Bondi, J., and Wiles, J. 1986. School reform in Florida: Implications for the middle school. *Educational Leadership* 44:44–46.

Bowles, S., and Gintis, H. 1983. IQ in the United States class structure. In *The hidden curriculum and moral education*, edited by H. Giroux and D. Purpel, 229–66. Berkeley: McCutchan Publishing.

Boykin, A.W. 1979. Psychological/behavioral verve: Some theoretical explorations and empirical manifestations. In *Research directions of black psychologists*, edited by A.W. Boykin; A.J. Franklin; and J.F. Yates, 351–67. New York: Russell Sage Foundation.

Boykin, A.W. 1986. The triple quandary and the schooling of Afro-American children. In *The school achievement of minority children*, edited by U. Neisser, 57–92. Hillsdale, N.J. : Lawrence Erlbaum Associates.

Boykin, A.W., and Allen, B.A. 1986, Fall. *Towards a heuristic investigation into black culture*. Paper presented at the Emory Cognition and Education Conference, Atlanta, Ga.

Bracey, G.W. 1986. Pandora and the pollyanna: Some comments on "the rush to mandate." *Phi Delta Kappan* 67:452–55.

Brandt, G.L. 1986. *The realization of anti-racist teaching*. London: Taylor and Francis.

Branson, H.R. 1987. The hazards in black higher education: Program and commitment needs. *The Journal of Negro Education* 56:129–36.

Brantlinger, E. 1985. Low-income parents' perceptions of favoritism in the schools. *Urban Education* 20:82–102.

Brattesani, K.A.; Weinstein, R.S.; and Marshall, H.H. 1984. Student perceptions of differential teacher treatment as moderators of teacher expectation effects. *Journal of Educational Psychology* 76:236–47.

Braun, C. 1976. Teacher expectations: Sociopsychological dynamic. *Review of Educational Research* 46:185–213.

Braxton, M.V. and Bullock, C.S. 1972. Teacher partiality in desegregation. *Integrated Education* 10:42–46.

Brookover, W.B. 1985. Can we make schools effective for minority students? *Journal of Negro Education* 54:257–68.

Brophy, J.E. 1981. Teacher praise: A functional analysis. *Review of Educational Research* 51:5–32.

———. 1982. Successful teaching strategies for the inner-city child. *Phi Delta Kappan* 63:527–30.

———. 1983. Research on the self-fulfilling prophecy and teacher expectations. *Journal of Educational Psychology* 75:633–61.

———. 1985. Teacher-student interactions. In *Teacher expectancies*, edited by J.B. Dusek, 303–28. Hillsdale, N.J. : Lawrence Erlbaum Associates.

Brophy, J., and Evertson, C.M. 1981. *Student characteristics and teaching*. New York: Longman Press.

Brophy, J., and Good, T. 1970. Teachers' communications of differential expectations for children's classroom performance: Some behavioral data. *Journal of Educational Psychology* 61:356–74.

———. 1974. *Teacher-student relationships: Causes and consequences*. New York: Holt, Rinehart and Winston.

Brown, A.L.; Palincsar, A.S.; and Purcell, L. 1986. Poor readers: Teach, don't label. In *The school achievement of minority children*, edited by U. Neisser, 105–43. Hillsdale, N.J. : Lawrence Erlbaum Associates.

Brown, T.J. 1986. *Teaching minorities more effectively*. Lanham, Md. : University Press of America.

Brown, W.; Payne, L.; Lankewich, L.; and Cornell, J. 1970. Praise, criticism, and race. *Elementary School Journal* 70:373–77.

Bruno, J.E., and Doscher, M.L. 1981. Contributing to the harms of racial isolation: Analysis of requests for teacher transfers in a large urban school district. *Educational Administration Quarterly* 17:93–108.

Byalick, R., and Bersoff, D.N. 1974. Reinforcement practices of black and white teachers in integrated classrooms. *Journal of Educational Psychology* 66:473–80.

Byers, P., and Byers, H. 1972. Non-verbal communication in the education of children. In *Function of language in the classroom*, edited by C. Cazden, V. John, and D. Hymes, 3–31. New York: Teachers College Press.

Campbell, P.B.; Gardner, J.A.; and Seitz, P. 1982. *High school vocational graduates: Which doors are open?* Columbus, Ohio: Ohio State University.

Carnegie Corporation of New York. 1984/1985. Renegotiating society's contract with the public schools. *Carnegie Quarterly* 29/30:1–4, 6–11.

"Carnegie Forum on Education." 1986. *A nation prepared: Teachers for the 21st century*. New York.

Chance, P. 1986. *Thinking in the classroom*. New York: Teachers College Press.

The Children's Defense Fund. 1985. *Black and white children in America: Key facts*. Washington, D.C.

_____. 1987. *The Children's Time*. Washington, D.C.

Chion-Kenney, L. 1984, November 7. Educators warned that reform may peril minority-student gains. *Education Week* 4:8.

Clark, D.L.; Lotto, L.S.; and McCarthy, M.M. 1980. Factors associated with success in urban elementary schools. *Phi Delta Kappan* 61:467–70.

Clark, R.M. 1983. *Family life and school achievement: Why poor black children succeed or fail*. Chicago: University of Chicago Press.

Coates, B. 1972. White adult behavior toward black and white children. *Child Development* 43:143–54.

Coates, J.F., and Jarratt, J. 1987. *Future search: Forces and factors shaping education*. Washington, D.C. : National Educational Association.

Cole, B.P. 1986. The black educator: An endangered species. *Journal of Negro Education* 55:326–34.

Coleman, J. 1966. *Equality of educational opportunity*. Washington, D.C. : Office of Education.

The College Board. 1985. *Equality and excellence: The educational status of black Americans*. New York.

Combs, A.W. 1979. *Myths in education: Beliefs that hinder progress and their alternatives*. Boston: Allyn and Bacon.

Comer, J.P. 1986. Parent participation in the schools. *Phi Delta Kappan* 67:442–46.

Cooke, B.G. 1972. Nonverbal communication among Afro-Americans: An initial classification. In *Rappin' and stylin' out*, edited by T. Kochman, 32–64. Urbana: University of Illinois Press.

Cooper, C.C. 1988. Implications of the absence of black teachers/administrators on black youth. *Journal of Negro Education* 57:123–24.

Cooper, H.M. 1985. Models of teacher expectation communication. In *Teacher expectancies*, edited by J.B. Dusek, 135–58. Hillsdale, N.J. : Lawrence Erlbaum Associates.

Cooper, H.M., and Good, T.L. 1983. *Pygmalion grows up: Studies in the expectation communication process*. New York: Longman Press.

Cornbleth, C., and Korth, W. 1980. Teacher perceptions and teacher-student interaction in integrated classrooms. *Journal of Experimental Education* 48:259–63.

Coursen, D. 1975. *Women and minorities in administration*. Arlington, Va. : National Association of Elementary School Principals.

Crain, R.L. 1976. Why academic research fails to be useful. *School Review* 84:337–51.

Crandall, V.C.; Katkovsky, W.; and Crandall, V.J. 1965. Children's beliefs in their own control of reinforcements in intellectual-academic situations. *Child Development* 36:91–104.

Crawford, J., and Viadero, D. 1986, September 24. Study examines at risk black, Hispanic students. *Education Week* 6:10.

Cruickshank, D.R. 1985. Profile of an effective teacher. In *Education 87–88*, edited by F. Schultz, 216–21. Guilford, Conn. : Dushkin Publishing.

Csikszentmihalyi, M., and McCormack, J. 1986. The influence of teachers. *Phi Delta Kappan* 67:415–19.

Cureton, G.O. 1978. Using a black learning style. *The Reading Teacher* 31(7):751–56.

Damico, S.B., and Scott, E. 1985, March. *Comparison of black and white females' behavior in elementary and middle schools*. Paper presented at the meeting of the American Educational Research Association, Chicago.

Datta, L.; Schaefer, E.; and Davis, M. 1968. Sex and scholastic aptitude as variables in teachers' rating of the adjustment and classroom behaviors of Negro and other seventh-grade students. *Journal of Educational Psychology* 59:94–101.

Dillard, J.L. 1977. *Lexicon of black English*. New York: Seabury Press.

Durkin, D. 1984. Poor black children who are successful readers. *Urban Education* 19:53–76.

Dusek, J.B., ed. 1985. *Teacher expectancies*. Hillsdale, N.J. : Lawrence Erlbaum Associates.

Dusek, J.B., and Joseph, G. 1985. The bases of teacher expectancies. In *Teacher expectancies*, edited by J.B. Dusek, 229–50. Hillsdale, N.J. : Lawrence Erlbaum Associates.

Dweck, C.S., and Bush, E.S. 1976. Sex differences in learned helplessness: Differential debilitation with peer and adult evaluators. *Developmental Psychology* 12:147–56.

Dyer, H.S. 1980. *Parents can understand testing*. Columbia, Md. : The National Committee for Citizens in Education.

Eaves, R.C. 1975. Teacher race, student race, and behavior problem checklist. *Journal of Abnormal Child Psychology* 70:979–87.

Edelman, M.W. 1986. Save the children. *Ebony* 41:53–58.

Edmonds, R. 1979. Effective schools for the urban poor. *Educational Leadership* 37:15–23.

_____. 1986. Characteristics of effective schools. In *The school achievement of minority children*, edited by U. Neisser, 93–104. Hillsdale, N.J. : Lawrence Erlbaum Associates.

Edwards, C.E. 1981. Are black administrators an endangered species? *Lifeline* 1:1–2.

Edwards, P.A. 1987. Working with families from diverse backgrounds. In *Educating black children: America's challenge*, edited by D.S. Strickland and E.J. Cooper, 92–104. Washington, D.C. : Howard University Press.

Emihovich, C.A. 1983. The color of misbehaving: Two case studies of deviant boys. *Journal of Black Studies* 13:259–74.

Ethridge, S.B. 1979. The impact of the 1954 Brown vs. Topeka Board of Education decision on black educators. *The Negro Educational Review* 30:217–32.

Eubanks, E.E., and Levine, D.U. 1987. Administrative and organizational arrangements and considerations in the effective schools movement. In *Educating black children: America's challenge*, edited by D.S. Strickland and E.J. Cooper, 19–32. Washington, D.C. : Howard University Press.

Eyler, J.; Cook, V.; and Ward, L. 1982, March. *Resegregation: Segregation within desegregated schools*. Paper presented at the meeting of the American Education Research Association, New York.

Feldman, R.S., and Orchowsky, S. 1979. Race and performance of students as determinants of teacher nonverbal behavior. *Contemporary Educational Psychology* 4:324–33.

Felsenthal, H. 1970, March. *Sex differences in teacher-pupil interaction in first grade reading instruction*. Paper presented at the meeting of the American Educational Research Association, Minneapolis.

Feshbach, N.D. 1969. Student teacher preferences for elementary pupils varying in personality characteristics. *Journal of Educational Psychology* 60:126–32.

Findley, W., and Bryan, M. 1975. *The pros and cons of ability grouping*. Washington, D.C. : National Education Association.

Fine, M. 1988. De-institutionalizing educational equity. In *School success for students at risk*, edited by Council of Chief State School Officers, 89–119. Orlando: Harcourt Brace Jovanovich.

Fleming, J. 1984. *Blacks in college*. San Francisco: Jossey-Bass.

Fordham, S., and Ogbu, J.U. 1986. Black students' school success: Coping with the "burden of 'acting white.' " *The Urban Review* 18:176–206.

Foster, H.L. 1974. *Ribbin', jivin', and playin' the dozens: The unrecognized dilemma of inner city schools*. Cambridge, Mass. : Ballinger Publishing.

Freedman, D.G. 1974. *Human infancy: An evolutionary perspective*. Hillsdale, N.J.: Lawrence Erlbaum Associates.

Freire, P. 1970. *Pedagogy of the oppressed*. New York: Herder and Herder.

Futrell, M.H., and Robinson, S.P. 1986. Testing teachers: An overview of NEA's position, policy, and involvement. *Journal of Negro Education* 55:397–404.

Gallup, G.H. 1986. The 18th annual Gallup poll of the public's attitudes toward the public schools. *Phi Delta Kappan* 68:43–59.

Garibaldi, A.M. 1986. *The decline of teacher production in Louisiana (1976–83) and attitudes toward the profession*. Atlanta: Southern Education Foundation.

———. 1988. *Educating black male youth: A moral and civic imperative*. New Orleans: New Orleans Public Schools.

Gersten, R., and Keating, T. 1987. Long-term benefits from direct instruction. *Educational Leadership* 44:28–31.

Getting tough. 1988, February 1. *Time*, pp. 52–58.

Gilmore, P. 1985. "Gimme room": School resistance, attitude, and access to literacy. *Journal of Education* 167:111–28.

Ginzberg, E.; Berliner, H.S.; and Ostow, M. 1988. *Young people at risk: Is prevention possible?* Boulder, Colo. : Westview Press.

Giroux, H., and Penna, A. 1983. Social education in the classroom: The dynamics of the hidden curriculum. In *The Hidden Curriculum and Moral Education*, edited by H. Giroux and D. Purpel, 100–121. Berkeley: McCutchan Publishing.

Glenn, B.C. 1981. *What works? An examination of effective schools for poor black children*. Cambridge, Mass. : Center for Law and Education.

Good, T. 1970. Which pupils do teachers call on? *Elementary School Journal* 70:190–98.

Good, T.L. 1981. Teacher expectations and student perceptions: A decade of research. *Educational Leadership* 38:415–22.

Good, T., and Brophy, J. 1978. *Looking in classrooms*. New York: Harper and Row.

Good, T., and Dembo, M. 1973. Teacher expectations: Self-report data. *School Review* 81:247–53.

Goodlad, J. 1984. *A place called school*. New York: McGraw-Hill.

Gordon, I., and Breivogel, W.F. 1976. *Building effective home-school relationships*. Boston: Allyn and Bacon.

Gottlieb, D. 1964. Teaching and students: The views of Negro and white teachers. *Sociology of Education* 37:345–53.

Gouldner, H. 1978. *Teachers' pets, troublemakers, and nobodies: Black children in elementary school*. Westport, Conn. : Greenwood Press.

Grant, L. 1984. Black females' "place" in desegregated classrooms. *Sociology of Education* 57:98–111.

_____. 1985. Race-gender status, classroom interaction, and children's socialization in elementary school. In *Gender and Classroom Interaction*, edited by L.C. Wilkerson and C.B. Marrett, 57–77. Orlando, Fla. : Academic Press.

_____. 1986, April. *Classroom peer relationships of minority and nonminority students*. Paper presented at the meeting of the American Educational Research Association, San Francisco.

Greer, C. 1972. *The great school legend: A revisionist interpretation of American public education*. New York: Basic Books.

Griffin, A.R., and London, C.B.G. 1980. Student relations among inner city teachers: A comparative study by teacher race. *Education* 101:139–47.

Guskey, T.R. 1986. Staff development and the process of teacher change. *Educational Researcher* 15:5–12.

Guskin, J. 1970, March. *The social perception of language variations: Black dialect and expectation of ability*. Paper presented at the meeting of the American Educational Research Association, Minneapolis.

Hale-Benson, J.E. 1986. *Black children: Their roots, culture, and learning styles*. 2d ed. Baltimore: Johns Hopkins University Press.

Hall, V.C., and Merkel, S.P. 1985. Teacher expectancy effects and educational psychology. In *Teacher expectancies*, edited by J.B. Dusek, 67–92. Hillsdale, N.J. : Lawrence Erlbaum Associates.

Hallinan, M.T., and Sorensen, A.B. 1983. The formation and stability of instructional groups. *American Sociological Review* 48:838–51.

Hamilton, S.F. 1983. The social side of schooling: Ecological studies of classrooms and schools. *Elementary School Journal* 83:313–34.

Haney, J.E. 1978. The effects of the Brown decision on black education. *Journal of Negro Education* 47:88–95.

Hanna, J.L. 1988. *Disruptive school behavior: Class, race, and culture*. New York: Holmes and Meier.

Hare, B.R., and Castenell, L.A. 1985. No place to run, no place to hide: Comparative status and future prospects of black boys. In *Beginnings: The social and affective development of black children*, edited by M.B. Spencer, G.K. Brookins, and W.R. Allen, 201–14. Hillsdale, N.J. : Lawrence Erlbaum Associates.

Harvey, D.G., and Slavin, G.T. 1975. The relationship between SES and teacher expectation. *Social Forces* 54:140–59.

Hawley, W.D. 1986. Toward a comprehensive strategy for addressing the teacher shortage. *Phi Delta Kappan* 67:712–18.

Hawley, W.D.; Rosenholtz, S.J.; with Goodstein, H., and Hasselbring, T. 1984a. Effective teaching. *Peabody Journal of Education* 61:15–52.

_____. 1984b. Parent involvement and assistance. *Peabody Journal of Education* 61:117–24.

_____. 1984c. School leadership and student learning. *Peabody Journal of Education* 61:53–83.

Heath, S.B. 1982. Questioning at home and at school: A comparative study. In *Doing ethnography: Educational anthropology in action*, edited by G. Spindler, 102–31. New York: Holt, Rinehart, and Winston.

_____. 1983. Research currents: A lot of talk about nothing. *Language Arts* 60:999–1007.

Henderson, A.T., ed. 1987. *The evidence grows: Parent involvement improves student achievement*. Columbia, Md. : National Committee for Citizens in Education.

Herskovits, M.J. 1958. *The myth of the Negro past*. Boston: Beacon Press.

Hilliard, A.G. 1988. Public support for successful instructional practices for at-risk students. In *School success for students at risk*, edited by Council of Chief State School Officers, 195–208. Orlando: Harcourt Brace Jovanovich.

_____. 1983. Psychological factors associated with language in the education of the African-American child. *Journal of Negro Education* 52:24–34.

Hillman, S.B., and Davenport, G.G. 1978. Teacher-student interactions in desegregated schools. *Journal of Educational Psychology* 70:545–53.

Hodgkinson, H. 1988. The right schools for the right kids. *Educational Leadership* 45:10–14.

Holliday, B.G. 1985. Differential effects of children's self-perceptions and teachers' perceptions of black children's academic achievement. *Journal of Negro Education* 54:71–81.

Honig, B. 1987. High standards and great expectations: The foundations for student achievement. In *Educating black children: America's challenge*, edited by D.S. Strickland and E.J. Cooper, 11–18. Washington, D.C. : Howard University Press.

Hood, J.F. 1984. *Update on the school market for microcomputers*. Westport, Conn. : Market Data Retrieval.

Hoover-Dempsey, K.V.; Bassler, O.C.; and Brissie, J.S. 1987. Parent involvement: Contributions of teacher efficacy, school socio-economic status, and other school characteristics. *American Educational Research Journal* 24:417–35.

Houlton, D. 1986. *Cultural diversity in the primary school*. London: B.T. Balsford, Ltd.

Howard, J., and Hammond, R. 1985. Rumors of inferiority. *The New Republic* 193:17–21.

Howe, F. 1971. Teacher perception toward the learning ability of students from different racial and socio-economic backgrounds. (Doctoral dissertation, Michigan State University.) *Dissertation Abstracts International* 31:5847A.

Hutt, C. 1979. Why do girls underachieve? *Trends in Education* 4:24–28.

Ianni, F.A.J. 1987. Revisiting school-community responsibilities in the administration of education. In *Educating black children: America's challenge*, edited by D.S. Strickland and E.J. Cooper, 2–18. Washington, D.C. : Howard University Press.

Irvine, J.J. 1985, March. *The accuracy and stability of teachers' achievement expectations as related to students' race and sex*. Paper presented at the meeting of the American Educational Research Association, Chicago.

_____. 1986. Teacher-student interactions: Effects of student race, sex, and grade level. *Journal of Educational Psychology* 78:14–21.

_____. 1988a. Disappearing black educators. *Elementary School Journal* 88:503–13.

_____. 1988c. Urban schools that work: A summary of relevant factors. *Journal of Negro Education* 57:236–42.

_____. 1988b, April. *Teacher race as a factor in black students' achievement.* Paper presented at the meeting of the American Educational Research Association, New Orleans.

Irvine, J.J., and Irvine, R.W. 1980. A reassessment of racial balance remedies. *Phi Delta Kappan* 62:180–81.

Irvine, R.W., and Irvine, J.J. 1983. The impact of the desegregation process on the education of black students: Key variables. *The Journal of Negro Education* 52:410–22.

Jackson, G., and Cosca, C. 1974. The inequality of educational opportunity in the Southwest: An observational study of ethnically mixed classrooms. *American Journal of Educational Research* 11:219–29.

Jackson, P., and Lahaderne, H. 1967. Inequalities of teacher-pupil contacts. *Psychology in the Schools* 4:204–11.

Jackson, P.W. 1983. The daily grind. In *The hidden curriculum and moral education,* edited by H. Giroux and D. Purpel, 28–60. Berkeley: McCutchan Publishing.

Jago, A.G. 1982. Leadership: Perspectives in theory and research. *Management Science* 28:315–36.

Jencks, C.; Smith, M.; Acland, H.; Bone, M.J.; Cohen, D.; Gintis, H.; Ueyns, B.; and Michelson, S. 1972. *Inequality: A reassessment of the effect of family and schooling in America.* New York: Harper Colophon.

Johnson, C.S. 1954. Some significant social and educational implications of the U.S. Supreme Court's decision. *Journal of Negro Education* 23:364–71.

Johnson, S.T., and Prom-Jackson, S. 1986. The memorable teacher: Implications for teacher selection. *The Journal of Negro Education* 55:272–83.

Jones, E.H., and Montenegro, X.P. 1988. *Women & minorities in school administration.* Arlington, Va. : American Association of School Administrators.

Jones, F.C. 1981. *A traditional model of educational excellence.* Washington, D.C. : Howard University Press.

Jones, J.D.; Van Fossen, B.E.; and Spade, J.Z. 1987, April. *Individual and organizational predictors of high school track placement.* Paper presented at the meeting of the American Educational Research Association, Washington, D.C.

Jussim, L. 1986. Self-fulfilling prophecies: A theoretical and integrative review. *Psychological Review* 93:429–45.

Kash, M.M., and Borich, G.D. 1978. *Teacher behavior and pupil self-concept.* Reading, Mass. : Addison-Wesley.

Katz, M. 1973, February. *Attitudinal modernity, classroom power and status characteristics: An investigation.* Paper presented at the meeting of the American Educational Research Association, New Orleans.

Kedar-Voivodas, G. 1983. The impact of elementary children's school roles and sex roles on teacher attitudes: An interactional analysis. *Review of Educational Research* 53:415–37.

Kleinfeld, J. 1972. The relative importance of teachers and parents in the formation of Negro and white students' academic self-concept. *The Journal of Educational Research* 65:211–12.

Kochman, T. 1981. *Black and white styles in conflict*. Chicago: University of Chicago Press.

Kohn, A. 1986. *No contest: The case against competition*. New York: Houghton Mifflin.

Kottkamp, R.B.; Provenzo, E.F.; and Cohn, M.M. 1986. Stability and change in a profession: Two decades of teacher attitudes, 1964–1984. *Phi Delta Kappan* 67:559–67.

Krupczak, W.P. 1972. Relationships among student self-concept of academic ability, teacher perception of student academic ability and student achievement. (Doctoral dissertation, University of Miami.) *Dissertation Abstracts International* 33:3388A.

Labov, W. 1970. The logic of nonstandard English. In *Language and poverty: Perspectives on a theme*, edited by F. Williams, 153–89. Chicago: Markham Publishing.

———. 1972. *Language in the inner city*. Philadelphia: University of Pennsylvania Press.

Leacock, E. 1969. *Teaching and learning in city schools: A comparative study*. New York: Basic Books.

Lee, C.C. 1984. An investigation of psychosocial variables related to academic success for rural black adolescents. *Journal of Negro Education* 53:424–34.

Lefkowitz, L.J. 1972. Ability grouping: De facto segregation in the classroom. *Clearing House* 46:293–97.

Leinhardt, G.; Seewald, A.; and Engel, M. 1979. Learning what's taught: Sex differences in instruction. *Journal of Educational Psychology* 71:432–39.

Levin, H.M. 1987. Accelerated schools for disadvantaged students. *Educational Leadership* 44:19–21.

Levine, D.V.; Levine, R.R.; and Eubanks, E.E. 1985. Successful implementation of instruction at inner-city schools. *The Journal of Negro Education* 54:313–32.

Levy, J. 1983. Research synthesis on right and left brain hemispheres: We think with both sides of the brain. *Educational Leadership* 40:66–71.

Lewis, D.K. 1975. The black family: Socialization and sex roles. *Phylon* 36:221–37.

Lietz, J. and Gregory, M. 1978. Pupil race and sex determinants of office and exceptional educational referral. *Educational Research Quarterly* 2:61–66.

Lightfoot, S.L. 1976. Socialization and education of young black girls in school. *Teachers College Record* 78:239–62.

———. 1978. *Worlds apart: Relationships between families and schools*. New York: Basic Books.

———. 1981. Toward conflict resolution: Relationships between families and schools. *Theory Into Practice* 20:97–104.

Lippitt, R., and Gold, M. 1959. Classroom social structure as a mental health problem. *Journal of Social Issues* 15:40–49.

Lomotey, K., and Brookins, C.C. 1988. Independent black school institutions: A cultural perspective. In *Visible now: Blacks in private schools*, edited by D.T. Slaughter and D.J. Johnson, 163–83. Westport, Conn. : Greenwood Press.

Longstreet, W.C. 1978. *Aspects of ethnicity*. New York: Teachers College Press.

Lubeck, S. 1985. *The sandbox society*. London: Falmer Press.

Martin, R. 1972. Student sex and behavior as determinants of the type and frequency of teacher-student contacts. *Journal of School Psychology* 10:339–47.

Mazzarella, J.A. 1981. Portrait of a leader. In *School leadership: Handbook for survival*, edited by S.C. Smith, J.A. Mazzarella, and P.K. Piele, 17–36. Eugene, Oreg. : University of Oregon.

McAdoo, H.P. 1981. *Black families*. Beverly Hills: Sage Publications.

McDill, E. 1986. *Raising standards and retaining students: The impact of the reform recommendations on potential dropouts*. Baltimore: Johns Hopkins University.

McTighe, J., and Schollenberger, J. 1985. The need to improve student thinking: A rationale statement. *Developing and improving student thinking abilities*. Baltimore, Md. : The Maryland Department of Education.

Merton, R.K. 1957. *Social theory and social structure*. New York: Free Press.

Metz, M.H. 1978. *Classrooms and corridors*. Berkeley, Calif. : University of California Press.

Meyer, W., and Lindstrom, D. 1969. *The distribution of teacher approval and disapproval of Head Start children*. Washington, D.C. : Office of Economic Opportunity.

Meyer, W., and Thompson, G. 1956. Teacher interaction with boys as contrasted with girls. *Journal of Educational Psychology* 47:385–97.

Milner, M. 1972. *The illusion of equality*. San Francisco: Jossey-Bass.

National Alliance of Black School Educators. 1984. *Saving the African American child*. Washington, D.C.

National Assessment of Educational Progress. 1985. *The reading report card*. (Report No. 15-R-01). Princeton, N.J. : Educational Testing Service.

National Center for Education Statistics. 1982. *High school and beyond*. Washington, D.C.

National Coalition of Advocates for Students. 1987. *A special analysis of 1984 elementary and secondary school civil rights survey data*. Boston.

National Commission on Excellence. 1983. *A nation at risk*. Washington, D.C.

National Committee for Citizens in Education. 1985. *Parent rights card*. Columbia, Md.

———. 1987. *Annual Education Checkup*. Columbia, Md.

Nevi, C. 1987. In defense of tracking. *Educational Leadership* 44:24–26.

Nicholls, J.G. 1975. Causal attributions and other achievement-related cognitions: Effects of task outcomes, attainment value, and sex. *Journal of Personality and Social Psychology* 31:379–89.

Nie, H.H., Hull, C.H. Jenkins, J.G., Steinbrenner, K., and Bent, D.H. 1985. *Statistical package for the social sciences*. New York: McGraw-Hill.

Oakes, J. 1985. *Keeping track: How schools structure inequality*. New Haven: Yale University Press.

———. 1986. Keeping track, part 2: Curriculum inequality and school reform. *Phi Delta Kappan* 68:148–53.

———. 1988. Tracking in mathematics and science education: A structural contribution to unequal schooling. In *Class, race, and gender in American education*, edited by L. Weis, 106–25. Albany: State University of New York Press.

Ogbu, J. 1974. *The next generation: An ethnography of education in an urban neighborhood*. New York: Academic Press.

———. 1978. *Minority education and caste: The American system in cross-cultural perspective*. New York: Academic Press.

———. 1988b. Cultural diversity and human development. In *Black children and poverty: A developmental perspective*, edited by D.T. Slaughter, 11–28. San Francisco: Jossey-Bass.

———. 1988a. Class stratification, racial stratification, and schooling. In *Class, race, and gender in American education*, edited by L. Weis, 163–82. Albany: State University of New York Press.

Orr, E.W. 1987. *Twice as less: Black English and the performance of black students in mathematics and science*. New York: Norton.

Owens, R.G. 1987. *Organizational behavior in education*. Englewood Cliffs, N.J. : Prentice-Hall.

Pallas, A.M., Natriello, G., and McDill, E.L. 1989. The changing nature of the disadvantaged population: Current dimensions and future trends. *Educational Researcher*, 18:16–22.

Pasteur, A.B., and Toldson, I.L. 1982. *The roots of soul: The psychology of black expressiveness*. New York: Anchor Press.

Peck, R.F.; Manning, B.A.; and Buntain, D. 1977. *The impact of teacher and student characteristics on student self-concept: A review of research*. Austin, Tex. : University of Texas.

Persell, C.H. 1977. *Education and inequality*. New York: Free Press. Arlington, VA. : American Association of School Administrators.

Perspectives on racial minority and women school administrators. 1983. Arlington, VA.: American Association of School Administrators.

Peters, M.F. 1981. "Making it" black family style: Building on the strengths of the black family. In *Family strengths three: Roots of well-being*, edited by N. Stinnett, J. DeFrain, K. King, P. Knaub, and G. Rowe, 73–91. Lincoln: University of Nebraska Press.

Picott, R. 1976. *A quarter of a century of elementary and secondary education*. Washington, D.C. : Association for the Study of Negro Life and History.

Racial and ethnic makeup of college and university enrollments. 1986, July 23. *The Chronicle of Higher Education* 32:25.

Ramírez, M., and Castañeda, A. 1974. *Cultural democracy, bicognitive development, and education*. New York: Academic Press.

Revicki, D.A. 1981. *The relationship among socioeconomic status, home environment, parent involvement, child self-concept, and child achievement*. (ERIC Document Reproduction Service No. ED 206 645.)

Rich, D. 1987. *Teachers and parents: An adult-to-adult approach*. Washington, D.C. : National Education Association.

Rist, R.C. 1970. Student social class and teacher expectations: The self-fulfilling prophecy and ghetto education. *Harvard Educational Review* 40:411–51.

_____. 1973. *The urban school: A factory for failure*. Cambridge, Mass. : MIT Press.

_____. 1987. Do teachers count in the lives of children? *Educational Researcher* 16:41–42.

Rodman, B. 1985, November 20. Teaching's "endangered species." *Education Week* 5:11–12.

Rosenbaum, J. 1976. *Making inequality: The hidden curriculum of high school tracking*. New York: Wiley.

Rosenthal, R., and Jacobson, L. 1968. *Pygmalion in the classroom: Teacher expectation and pupils' intellectual development*. New York: Holt, Rinehart and Winston.

Rosser, P. 1989. *The SAT gender gap: Identifying the causes*. Washington, D.C. : Center for Women's Policy Studies.

Rothman, R. 1987, September 30. Students' scores on college test remain stable. *Education Week* 7:1, 19.

Rotter, J.C.; Robinson, E.H., and Fey, M.A. 1987. *Parent-teacher conferencing*. Washington, D.C. : National Education Association.

Rowan, B., and Miracle, A.W. 1983. Systems of ability grouping and the stratification of achievement in elementary schools. *Sociology of Education* 56:133–44.

Rubovits, P.C., and Maehr, M. 1973. Pygmalion black and white. *Journal of Personality and Social Psychology* 25:210–18.

Safilios-Rothschild, C. 1979. *Sex-role socialization and sex discrimination: A synthesis and critique of the literature.* Washington, D.C. : National Institute of Education.

Schiamberg, L.D. 1986, May. *The influence of family on educational and occupational achievement.* Paper presented at the meeting of The American Association for the Advancement of Science, Philadelphia, Pa.

Schofield, J.W. 1982. *Black and white in school: Trust, tension, and tolerance.* New York: Praeger.

Scott, M.B., and Ntegeye, M.G. 1980. Acceptance of minority student personality characteristics by black and white teachers. *Integrateducation* 18:110–12.

Seeman, M. 1975. Alienation studies. *Annual Review of Sociology* 1:91–123.

Seginer, R. 1983. Parents' educational expectations and children's academic achievement: A literature review. *Merrill-Palmer Quarterly* 29:1–23.

Sergiovanni, T.J.; Burlingame, M.; Coumbs, F.S.; and Thurston, P.W. 1980. *Educational governance and administration.* Englewood Cliffs, N.J. : Prentice-Hall.

Shade, B.J. 1982. Afro-American cognitive style: A variable in school success? *Review of Educational Research* 52:219–44.

Silberman, M. 1969. Behavioral expectations of teachers' attitudes toward elementary school students. *Journal of Educational Psychology* 60:402–7.

Simpson, A.W., and Erickson, M.T. 1983. Teachers' verbal and non-verbal communication patterns as a function of teacher race, student gender, and student race. *American Educational Research Journal* 20:183–98.

Sizemore, B.A. 1985. Pitfalls and promises of the effective school research. *Journal of Negro Education* 54:269–88.

Slavin, R.E. 1980. Cooperative learning in teams: State of the art. *Educational Psychologist* 15:93–111.

_____. 1982. *Cooperative learning: Student teams.* Washington, D.C. : National Education Association.

———. 1987a. Cooperative learning and the cooperative school. *Educational Leadership* 45:7–13.

_____. 1987b. Cooperative learning and the education of black students. In *Educating black children: America's challenge,* edited by D.S. Strickland and E.J. Cooper, Washington, D.C. : Howard University Press.

Slavin, R.E.; Karweit, N.L.; and Madden, N.A. 1989. *Effective programs for students at risk.* Needham Heights, Mass. : Allyn and Bacon.

Slavin, R.E., and Madden, N.A. 1979. School practices that improve race relations. *American Educational Research Journal* 16:169–80.

Slaughter, C.A. 1969. Cognitive style: Some implications for curriculum and instructional practices among Negro children. *Journal of Negro Education* 38:105–11.

Slaughter, D.T. 1986, April. *Children's peer acceptance and parental involvement in desegregated private elementary schools.* Paper presented at the meeting of the American Educational Research Association, San Francisco.

Smith, A.W. 1988. Maintaining the pipeline of black teachers for the twenty-first century. *Journal of Negro Education* 57:166–77.

Smith, E.J. 1982. The black female adolescent: A review of the educational, career and psychological literature. *Psychology of Women Quarterly* 6:261–88.

Smith, J.P. 1988. Tomorrow's white teachers: A response to the Holmes Group. *Journal of Negro Education* 57:178–94.

Smith, K.L., and Andrew, L.D. 1988, April. *An explanation of the beliefs, values, and attitudes of black students in Fairfax County.* Paper presented at the meeting of the American Educational Research Association, New Orleans, La.

Smitherman, G. 1977. *Talkin' and testifying.* Boston: Houghton Mifflin.

Snider, W. 1987, November 11. Study examines forces affecting racial tracking. *Education Week* 7:1, 20.

Snyder, M. 1982. Self-fulfilling stereotypes. *Psychology Today* 16:60–68.

Solomon, R.P. 1988. Black cultural forms in schools: A cross national comparison. In *Class, race, and gender in American education,* edited by L. Weis, 249–65. Albany: State University of New York Press.

Sowell, T. 1976. Patterns of black excellence. *The Public Interest* 43:26–58.

Spencer, M.B. 1983. Children's cultural values and parental child rearing strategies. *Developmental Review* 3:351–70.

St. John, N. 1971. Thirty-six teachers: Their characteristics and outcomes for black and white pupils. *American Educational Research Association* 8:635–48.

Stebbins, R.A. 1970. The meaning of disorderly behavior: Teacher definitions of a classroom situation. *Sociology of Education* 44:217–36.

Swap, S.M. 1987. *Enhancing parent involvement in schools: A manual for parents and teachers.* New York: Teachers College Press.

Tangri, S., and Moles, O. 1987. Parents and the community. In *Educators' handbook: A research perspective,* edited by V. Richardson-Koehler, New York: Longman.

Taylor, M.C. 1979. Race, sex, and the expression of self-fulfilling prophecies in a laboratory teaching situation. *Journal of Personality and Social Psychology* 37:897–912.

Taylor, M.C., and Foster, G.A. 1986. Bad boys and school suspension: Public policy implications for black males. *Sociological Inquiry* 56:498–506.

Trent, W. 1984. Equity considerations in higher education: Race and sex differences in degree attainment and major field from 1976 through 1981. *American Journal of Education* 92:280–305.

Twelve percent of U.S. families control 38% of wealth. 1986, July 19. *The Atlanta Constitution* 7:1, 14.

Vasquez, J.A. 1988. Contexts of learning from minority students. *The Educational Forum* 52:243–53.

W.T. Grant Foundation Commission on Work, Family, and Citizenship. 1988. *The Forgotten half: Non-college youth in America.* Washington, D.C.

Waetjen, W. 1962. Is learning sexless? *Education Digest* 28:12–14.

Walberg, H. 1984. Families as partners in educational productivity. *Phi Delta Kappan* 65:397–400.

Washington, V. 1980. Teachers in integrated classrooms: Profiles of attitudes, perceptions, and behavior. *The Elementary School Journal* 80:193–201.

_____. 1982. Racial differences in teacher perceptions of first and fourth grade pupils on selected characteristics. *The Journal of Negro Education* 51:60–72.

Weick, K.E. 1982. Administering education in loosely coupled schools. *Phi Delta Kappan* 63:673–76.

Weinstein, R.S. 1985. Student mediation of classroom expectancy effects. In *Teacher expectancies*, edited by J. Dusek, 329–50. Hillsdale, N.J. : Lawrence Erlbaum Associates.

Weis, L. 1985. *Between two worlds: Black students in an urban community college.* Boston: Routledge and Kegan Paul.

Welsh, P. 1986. *Tales out of school.* New York: Viking Penguin.

White, R. 1980. *Absent with cause, lessons of truancy.* London: Routledge, Kegan, Paul.

Wiggins, G. 1988, March 9. Ten radical suggestions for school reform. *Education Week* 8:28.

Wilkins, W.E. 1976. The concept of a self-fulfilling prophecy. *Sociology of Education* 49:175–83.

Williams, F. 1970. Psychological correlates of speech characteristics: On sounding "disadvantaged." *Journal of Speech and Hearing Research* 13:472–88.

Williamson, J.V. 1975. A look at black English. In *Ebonics: The true language of black folks*, edited by R.L. Williams, 11–23. St. Louis: Robert L. Williams and Associates.

Willis, S., and Brophy, J. 1974. Origins of teachers' attitudes toward young children. *Journal of Educational Psychology* 66:520–29.

Wilson, W.J. 1978. *The declining significance of race.* Chicago: University of Chicago Press.

Woodward, W.D., and Salzer, R.T. 1971. Black children's speech and teachers' evaluation. *Urban Education* 6:167–73.

Woolridge, P., and Richman, C. 1985. Teachers' choice of punishment as function of a student's gender, age, race, and IQ level. *Journal of School Psychology* 23:19–29.

Word, C.; Zanna, M.; and Cooper, J. 1974. The nonverbal mediation of self-fulfilling prophecies in interracial interaction. *Journal of Experimental Social Psychology* 10:109–20.

Wyche, L.G., and Wyche, J.M. 1984. Differences in teacher and parent perceptions of low income black children's home experiences. *The Negro Educational Review* 35:112–20.

Yee, A. 1968. Interpersonal attitudes of teacher and disadvantaged pupils. *Journal of Human Resources* 3:327–45.

Zwerling, L.S. 1976. *The crisis of the community college.* New York: McGraw-Hill.

Index

ABOUT THE AUTHOR

JACQUELINE JORDAN IRVINE is Associate Professor in the Division of Educational Studies at Emory University. She has written over thirty publications in the areas of women in school administration, gender and race equity, and instructional supervision. Presently she is developing training models for teachers of at-risk black students.